CBDCs: Work in Progress

An Introduction to Central Bank Digital Currencies

Russell Krueger
2023

With love and thanks to Sherlene, Elise, and Anna,

And our furry companions

Camille, Willow, and Taco

ISBN: 979-8-218-96169-5

CBDCs: Work in Progress

An Introduction to
Central Bank Digital Currencies

Contents

"WORK IN PROGRESS"

These words recognize that 100+ countries are now working to design and launch CBDCs.

The words also apply to this book which will be continually updated to keep up with the rapidly changing news about CBDCs.

This printing covers material through mid-July 2023.

I extend grateful thanks to Sherlene Lum, Gregg Forte, Ragheed Moghrabi, Ed Lehwald, and Syed Nadeem Adil for their astute reading and editorial guidance.

This study updates and generalizes to other regions the discussion of the digital euro CBDC in Krueger, *Building New Currency Unions: Lessons from the European Monetary Union* (2022).

CBDCs: Work in Progress

An Introduction to Central Bank Digital Currencies

RUSSELL KRUEGER

"Given the potentially far-reaching consequences of CBDCs, policy makers must apply the utmost prudence."
World Economic Forum (2020)

With over a hundred countries now issuing or investigating central bank digital currencies (CBDCs), this new type of financial instrument promises to reshape the international monetary system carrying with it broad and profound implications for monetary policy and economic behavior.[1]

The time has come for CBDCs to become part of the foundation of financial literacy. This study attempts to further that goal, introducing the history, characteristics, uses, and emerging issues of CBDCs for the benefit of students *(and their professors)* and the general public.

> *"I can tell you that we will see a very significant transformation that comes from CBDCs .... – Now there is an engagement, and for the right reason: the future has arrived."* Kristalina Georgieva, IMF Managing Director, May 1, 2023.[2]

---

[1] This study includes only publicly available information. A great deal of work on CBDCs is underway at international financial institutions (BIS, BIS Innovation Hubs, IMF, World Bank, BCBS, SWIFT, etc.) and many central banks and finance ministries. However, there is no feasible or objective way for the public to systematically capture all such information. To help keep up, students should monitor public sites such as the new IMF Fintech Note series, BIS.org, or https://www.ecb.europa.eu/paym/digital_euro/html/index.en.html to follow developing news about CBDCs.

[2] Strack (2023).

1

The CBDC story is global. This book likewise takes a global view to give an accurate picture of how CBDCs are used now and might be used in the future.[3]

From now on, every economics and finance student must become familiar with CBDCs, their impacts (both positive and negative), how they change policy, and how they might be regulated.

These experiments and investigations in combination with (1) a steady stream of country announcements about CBDCs, (2) news about recent severe disruptions and price volatility in private crypto markets ("crypto winter'), and (3) many legal and regulatory changes – create relevant news almost every week. *This book gives a picture as of mid-July 2023 – readers are advised to keep up-to-date with changes since then.*

As the story unfolds, students will learn about three major transformations of the global monetary and financial system – the digital cyber revolution that began with bitcoin and subsequently spawned thousands of financial innovations, the arrival of CBDCs during the past three years, and the new international agenda to build new legal and regulatory frameworks covering domestic and international use of digital assets. Taken together a new financial world is emerging. Although this book is focused on CBDCs, they cannot be understood without some grounding in the other elements of the digital revolution.[4]

---

[3] Chapters 3 and 4 describe CBDC projects in over 100 countries, including a deep dive into the important work underway in the 27 European Union countries. Chapters 5 looks at responses of the international finance community as it strives to better regulate both private and official digital financial instruments. Chapter 6 looks at some exciting projects (Aurum, Icebreaker, m-CBDC-Bridge, Nexus, and the IMF XC cross-border payments platform) that support cross-border transactions between countries' CBDC systems.

[4] A *lot* of crypto news has happened since the public start of the CBDC story around 2019 – 2020. And continues to happen. Despite many students' interest in such things, they are beyond the scope of this book.

This book will take the student to many different lands to learn about CBDCs. Whether you find the journey exciting or frightening, it is stuff you'll need to know.[5]

---

[5] An additional thought – Students, be sure to ask your professors how CBDCs will affect work in their fields!!

Chapter 1. What is a CBDC?

A CBDC is a new form of central bank money issued as a direct liability of a central bank as a digital equivalent of cash. It is an official obligation of a central bank in a digital form that takes advantage of the speed and efficiency of electronic instruments.

CBDCs are an important type of new digital financial instrument, but as will be seen they are just one part of the digital transformation of financial payment technology and infrastructure. Changes are massive and occurring rapidly.

CBDCs can be constructed either as;

- a *wholesale* instrument ('wCBDC') used between the central bank and financial intermediaries, *or*

- a general-purpose *retail* equivalent of cash ('rCBDC') for public use. An rCBDC can be operated directly by the central bank or in an intermediated two-tier system in which commercial banks handle the interface with the general public.

A wCBDC can be considered something like a digitized instrument representing the central bank's liability to fully cover the CBDC's value. As such, they are riskless assets tradable between financial institutions that provide access to innovative digital financial instruments and services. Their use could be cheaper and faster than existing transactions, provides settlement finality,[6] and is well-suited for cross-border transactions.

---

[6] Finality means that a transaction is legally finished when funds are paid/received. The recipient of an rCBDC can use it immediately after receiving it. Finality can speed monetary velocity – the speed at which a unit of money can be used for economic transactions. Settlement finality is an important feature offered by CBDCs that makes them similar to cash, but potentially faster.

An rCBDC, as a direct public claim on the central bank, can substitute for physical cash or deposit accounts at commercial banks. If an rCBDC gives similar or better services than cash or banks, it could reduce use of cash or result in disintermediation of banks, thereby affecting monetary and credit conditions or financial stability. rCBDCs could be direct competitors to cash, with impacts on cash behavior. Similarly, if rCBDCs can provide quick and inexpensive cross-border transactions, balance of payments flows can be affected, potentially unsettling financial conditions in both the CBDC selling and purchasing countries.[7][8]

rCBDCs can be operated directly by central banks or by 'two-tier systems' indirectly through a commercial technical platform or intermediated through banks and other private financial institutions with established financial ties with the public. The choice between these options can be challenging because their architectures and operating rules can significantly differ.

Central Bank Money

Central bank money is a central bank liability that can be used for settlement purposes. The essence of CBDCs is to create digital forms of

---

[7] Banks are 'financial intermediaries' that receive funds from one party (general public, businesses, governments, residents of other countries, etc.) and lend the funds to other parties. The intermediation function of banks can facilitate transactions between parties, safekeep funds, move funds into productive uses, and thus provide services to promote general economic benefit. However, if CBDCs divert funds away from banks ('disintermediation'), economic conditions can be unsettled, banks can face financial stress, and monetary policy actions could be impaired.

[8] Shifts of a country's CBDC into a neighboring country could create monetary and international payments problems in both countries. The management of cross-border CBDC flows is an important policy challenge. Some solutions are discussed in Chapter 6 below. Another solution is to create a monetary union that will operate with a single region-wide CBDC, which would be the situation of a future digital euro issued in the European Monetary Union.

central bank money that can be quickly traded by financial institutions and the public to support and settle financial transactions.

"The widespread use of central bank money for large and critical settlements is pivotal to the functioning of the global financial system, offering safety, availability, efficiency, neutrality, and finality." (Project mBridge 2022)

As easily transferrable riskless claims on the central bank, CBDCs are both monetary *and* payment instruments. The ability to use CBDCs within digital payments can help foster a new generation of rapid, low cost, and secure payment systems.[9]

A CBDC can be thought as a new form of 'central bank money'. Before the concept of CBDCs arose, central bank money comprised physical cash and reserve balances of banks at the central bank. Depending on the form taken, a CBDC could be a digital form of cash usable by the general public (rCBDC), or a new digital instrument used by the central bank and financial institutions (wCBDC).

---

[9] CBDCs can be viewed as a synthesis of money and payments instruments. The CBDC itself, as a digital claim on the central bank, can be thought of as a financial instrument usable as money. The arrangements by which CBDCs are sold or transferred between parties, how they are transmitted, how the funds involved are settled between parties, and how they are legally treated form the payments system for CBDCs. Many variants of CBDC payments systems are possible and can be expected to evolve rapidly by taking advantage of lack of default risk of CBDCs and their digital efficiencies. The relative effectiveness and cost of a country's payments system vs. CBDCs could be decisive in whether a CBDC scheme succeeds or fails.

This introduction focuses mostly on the CBDC rather than their payments systems. Payments systems are complex and often fall under different regulatory and legal frameworks from money. At this point, students do not need to delve deeply into payments systems, but should be aware that they will matter for better understanding the CBDC systems in specific countries or regions.

Commercial Bank Money vs CBDCs

Commercial bank money comprises the public's deposits at banks which are backed by the banks' reserves at the central bank. It usually consists of electronic entries in customers' bank accounts. It is 'money' because the public can use the deposits for transactions (for example, by withdrawing cash from the account or by writing a check to make a purchase) – and the public thinks of it as money.

Acceptance of rCBDCs could be inhibited if existing commercial bank money effectively serves the public (store of value, usefulness for transactions, high liquidity, simple person-to-person transfers, low processing costs, etc.). Conversely, if the CBDCs have superior attributes and become broadly accepted by the public, they could disrupt existing cash and bank money markets and institutions.

In economies with inefficient or expensive banking services, or have large populations lacking good access to banking services, CBDCs might be a path to more efficient financial markets and better banking services for broad swaths of the economy ('financial inclusion').

Many experiments are underway that test CBDC models and technical platforms. A small number of retail and wholesale CBDCs have been issued, which provides some early indications of trends and challenges. Work on CBDCs is moving very rapidly, and many institutional and legal/regulatory changes are in the works.

Defining money

The IMF's *Monetary and Financial Statistics Manual* (*MFSM*) defines money as financial instruments held for their usability as medium of exchange, store of value, or both. Moneyness is evaluated based on the extent the instruments provide liquidity and a store of nominal value.

'Broad Money' is the total of all liquid financial instruments held by money-holding sectors that are widely accepted in an economy as a medium of exchange, plus those that can be converted into a medium of

8

exchange at short notice at, or close to, their full nominal value. (¶s 6.10 – 6.12) Many types of instruments might be classified as part of Broad Money. (Box 6.1) In contrast, 'Narrow Money" comprises instruments (cash and rCBDCs) immediately available for use.

Broad Money is defined country-by-country based on national financial conditions and institutions.[10] For example, some countries include foreign currency deposits within Broad Money.[11]

The public's deposits at commercial banks are usually in Broad Money because some action (withdrawing funds, writing a check, or setting up an automatic payment scheme, etc.) is needed to access the funds.

Buying rCBDCs with cash does not change total Narrow Money because it simply switches one form of Narrow Money for another.[12] In contrast, buying rCBDCs by taking deposits from a commercial bank increases Narrow Money, but leaves total Broad Money unchanged (because the increase in rCBDCs is offset by the drop in deposits).

CBDCs come with risks. They could disrupt existing markets, upset monetary and balance of payments policies, might not fit into existing legal and regulatory systems, might be used for illegal purposes, could create threats to privacy, and have 'operational risks' of breaking down and severely damaging economic activity. A lot of attention is being paid to the potential macroeconomic risk of CBDCs to destabilize banking systems or create runs on exchange rates. Much of the current activity around CBDCs (including by the international financial community) is to identify and resolve the risks.

---

[10] Except in currency unions where all countries must use the same definition.

[11] Co-circulation means that a foreign currency (or foreign-currency deposits at banks) circulates alongside the domestic currency. (Krueger and Ha 1995).

[12] However. rCBDCs might be even more liquid than cash, thus changing the economic behavior of Narrow Money.

As simple as the idea of CBDCs as electronic versions of cash might seem, many issues – technical, legal, institutional, policy, and consumer protection – must be resolved. Creating a CBDC might be as complex as creating a physical currency. The complexity arises because crypto-assets can have features of cash, payment systems, securities, investment funds, or even commodities. They often fall outside of existing regulatory and tax rules. Legal jurisdiction over them (by country or by topic) often is unsettled.

Direct vs. Intermediated CBDCs *(per Auer and Böhme 2020)*

A **Direct CBDC** is run by the central bank which deals directly with customers. The CBDC is a liability of the central bank, which maintains the transactions ledger and has customer[13] information.

Three levels of 'intermediated' CBDCs are;

Hybrid CBDC – The CBDC is a liability of the central bank which maintains the customer ledger (like above), but banks distribute it.

Intermediated CBDC – The CBDC is a liability of the central bank, but the central bank only maintains a ledger of its wholesale transactions with banks, who distribute the CBDC to customers.

Indirect Architecture – The central bank maintains a wholesale ledger of transactions with banks. The instrument itself is a liability of the commercial bank; thus, it is similar to a stablecoin.[14]

Each type has a different architecture with different legal/regulatory implications. Policy and financial stability implications will also differ.

---

[13] Customer information might be known to the central bank, but it is possible to 'anonymize' the identity of the customer to the central bank.

[14] A stablecoin is a digital instrument designed to have a fixed value with another asset (currency, gold, other commodity, etc.). (See Chapter 2)

These uncertainties are heightened for cross-border transactions. International flows of CBDCs could be large, for tourism, cross-border income flows, remittances, capital flows, etc. Countries will need to adjust monetary and payment systems to handle such flows and monetary policy changes might follow. Ease of transacting in other countries' CBDCs might overwhelm smaller national currencies or result in other countries' CBDCs co-circulating within national cash systems or parallel to national CBDCs. All countries (including future unions) will need to consider how CBDCs could affect their systems and whether they should launch their own CBDC.[15]

Synthetic CBDCs

Retail CBDCs can take many forms. In a pure form they are direct liabilities of the central bank in a digital form. However, other options allow an entity other than the central bank to issue an instrument that effectively duplicates a CBDC. The entity could be semi-governmental or a private firm with the expertise and resources to create new digital financial instruments that serve many of the purposes of CBDCs.

In such cases, the central bank turns over tasks to other institutions to manage the system and issue the CBDC-like digital instruments. Instruments would be private liabilities, but backed up by holdings of central bank money that provide a de facto central bank guarantee.

A retail CBDC is complex and challenging. It might be easier and faster for the central bank to hand some tasks to existing effective banks and other financial institutions. (See Adrian 2019 or Project Aurum 2022)

Handling CBDC complexities might be beyond the resources of many small or medium-size countries, which argues for adoption of coordinated regional approaches or international standards and interoperational systems. This book covers multiple such initiatives.

---

[15] The cross-border aspects of CBDCs are significant and have led countries to adopt various strategies, including taking steps to prevent foreign CBDCs from entering as well as preventing nonresidents from holding the domestic CBDC.

It appears that CBDCs will become nearly universal in the next few years. Students, their professors, financial markets, government policy officials, businesses, and the general public will use them for the rest of their lives. Markets, institutions, policies, and laws will change. This book seeks to provide a sense of the forthcoming changes.

Keeping Account

CBDCs are reflected in central bank accounting records. wCBDCs are shown in positions between the central bank and banks or other authorized financial firms. rCBDCs are reflected in accounts with the general public (or perhaps with banks and other financial firms depending on how the system is set up).

Commercial banks place a percentage of deposits received from the public into reserves accounts at the central bank. The public's deposits at banks are part of the stock of Broad Money, backed by the banks' reserves at the central bank. Monetary policy involves taking actions to adjust money stock or reserves to promote policy goals (slow inflation, accelerate growth, etc.).

For rCBDCs sold to the general public, purchasers can withdraw funds from bank deposits to purchase the CBDCs. Lower deposits reduces the measured money stock, but purchasing the rCBDCs simultaneously increases that part of the money stock by an equal amount. Thus, Broad Money is unchanged.

The central bank's books, however, are changed. Banks' reserves at the central bank fall, but the central bank receives funds from the sale of the rCBDC. Different accounts in the central bank's books are used, the net of gains and losses might not be zero, and central bank income and expenses involved could change. Thus, the central bank needs to consider how rCBDCs could change both its own financial condition as well as commercial banks' finances.

Chapter 2. Digital Assets History and Terminology

A digital version of cash has long been a possibility[16], but new technologies have transformed and accelerated the likelihood. Several key developments (in roughly chronological order) help explain why CBDCs have emerged:

- *Bitcoin (2008)* – bitcoin was a breakthrough technical innovation that spurred many new instruments and market developments,
- *Altcoins (2011 and after),* digital 'alternative coins' that have different features than bitcoin,
- *Stablecoins (2014 and after),* which are altcoins often used for payments purposes that have value linked to a currency or basket of underlying items,
- *Smart contracts (2015 and after),* which are executable instructions written into cryptoassets to initiate transactions,
- *DeFi (decentralized finance) (2018 and after),* which builds on a bitcoin-type network to handle many banking and securities functions,
- *Libra (2019),* a stablecoin intended to directly challenge national currencies, and
- *EU actions (ongoing)* to encompass digital instruments within its regulatory framework. (The actions are covered in chapter 4.)

Following the stepping stones listed above, the public story on CBDCs began in 2019 and unfolded seriously only around 2020.

Beginning in mid-2022, turmoil and price collapses in private cryptoasset markets (called 'crypto winter') highlighted the need for riskless[17] digital assets such as CBDCs and led to accelerated international actions to create new rules and regulations for cryptoassets.

---

[16] For example, the European Union formally enacted rules of what it called 'e-money' as far back as 1998. (ECB 1998)

[17] 'Riskless' in this context means absence of default risk.

Bitcoin – How it all started

Bitcoin (market symbol BTC) began in 2008 following publication of the paper "Bitcoin: A Peer-to-Peer Electronic Cash System," authored under the pseudonym Satoshi Nakamoto. Bitcoin was designed as a fully anonymous financial instrument transferable by digital devices (computer, mobile phone, etc.) and outside of any government control.[18]

The term *'cryptocurrency'* was originally applied to bitcoin because its advocates argued that it was an anonymously traded (hence 'crypto' or secret) asset that could substitute for, or even replace, official national currency.[19] The term 'cryptocurrency' is often applied to other digital instruments as well, but neither bitcoin nor any other unofficial digital asset is a currency, 'crypto' or otherwise. *The term cryptocurrency is generally considered inaccurate and misleading – avoid using it.*

Such digital assets lack official backing, are often too volatile to be a stable store of value, are not in general use for transactions, have limited

---

[18] This section goes into some detail on bitcoin because it is currently the dominant digital asset and it established many practices related to cryptoassets. However, some later digital instruments (often called 'altcoins' or 'alternative coins') diverged from bitcoin in many different directions; only some can be discussed here.

[19] Early bitcoin advocates had many motivations (positive and negative) for embracing it. Price speculation certainly was part, but other desired attributes were to serve as a general transactions medium, maintain anonymity under repressive conditions, facilitate low-cost international transfers, serve as a store of value, and appeal to those with a technological bent, For some, bitcoin was seen as protection from possible collapse of fiat currencies and to overcome inflation concerns – ideas that aligned well for those espousing libertarian political views or 'Austrian economics' (*ask your professor*). On the dark side, bitcoin also facilitated illegal transactions, money laundering, and tax evasion. (Böhme et al 2015) A dozen years later, many are disappointed that some of the positive attributes advertised for bitcoin haven't materialized, but advocates still exist and bitcoin remains the single most important cryptoasset.

14

public acceptance, and with rare exceptions are not legal tender for use in official transactions such as for taxes. (In contrast, CBDCs are true digital currencies.)

Bitcoin mixes cash-like features (anonymous holding of value usable for transactions) and payment and settlement features (quick, low cost, verified transfers including international transfers). That mix allows it to be used for legitimate purposes as well as for tax avoidance and criminal activity.

Bitcoins can be used to transfer value quickly, inexpensively, and anonymously. They have no intrinsic value; their value is based on their acceptance by participants who hold and trade them. Bitcoin's price is based on supply and demand conditions – because the supply of bitcoins is strictly controlled (by the algorithm that generates them), changes in demand create volatile prices.[20]

Bitcoin operates through a global network of 'miners' (also called 'nodes' or 'validators'), which are independent data processing centers that can create new bitcoins by competing to solve a difficult mathematical computation or earn fees for verifying transactions (see text box Bitcoin Mining Income). Verified transactions are embedded in a permanent, encoded record of transactions called a 'blockchain.'[21]

---

[20] The supply of bitcoin available for trading is significantly less than cumulative total issuance because many are hoarded as stores of value and a good number have been lost.

[21] The bitcoin transaction verification system relies on majority votes by the global community of miners to avoid cases of spending a bitcoin (which is only a string of computer code) multiple times. Miners are compensated on a so-called *proof of work* basis by processing a large number of transactions and solving a very difficult mathematical problem. The process to communicate and verify globally is slow and takes 10 minutes or more to complete. Some new altcoin competitors to bitcoin have faster processing times, but bitcoin has remained the dominant cryptoasset.

(continued)

A key innovation of bitcoin was use of a digital "blockchain" that provides proof, verified by the bitcoin mining community, of who owns a coin. The system is designed so that a bitcoin cannot be owned simultaneously by more than one party and coin's owner cannot copy it and spend it more than once.

Bitcoin miners process transactions through 'distributed ledger technology' (DLT), in which encoded records of transactions are embedded in the blockchain and sent electronically to miners throughout the world to verify.[22] The system is described as 'permissionless', meaning that anyone willing to invest in and operate the required computer facilities can mine bitcoins for profit or set up exchanges that allow the public to buy, sell, or store bitcoins. A permissionless system requires a mechanism to review and approve transactions handled by individual miners – which increases the resources employed to verify transactions and slows processing.

The alternative is a 'permissioned' system operated by smaller groups of miners based on the size of their investment in the system or their authority (such as central banks).

Miners operate over the internet, which in principle allows them to be located anywhere in the world with internet service. The actual processing of transactions and creation of bitcoin involves a very large

---

Alternatively, verification can be done on a *proof of stake* basis that weights miner's votes based on the size of their investments (as measured by their capacity to process transactions, which is largely a function of the size of their investment in specialized computer chips). This system usually involves fewer miners and thus uses less energy. Verification might also be faster.

A third alternative is *proof of authority*, in which a few authorized and trusted verifiers (such as central banks) are used. These systems are fast and use much less energy than the original bitcoin model. A CBDC can operate on a proof of authority basis and thus can be much more efficient than private systems.

[22] Böhme et all (2015) has an informative introduction to DLT.

number of calculations requiring a vast amount of computer equipment. The installations generate huge amounts of heat that must be dissipated by air conditioning or by placing facilities in cold climates. The main cost of mining is the cost of electricity to run and cool the system, and thus processing is concentrated in areas of cheap electricity or cold temperatures (and accommodating regulatory regimes).

Bitcoin Mining Power Consumption

Globally, bitcoin mining uses more power than some countries. This demand for power has been widely criticized as environmentally damaging – excessive power demands were cited in 2021 among the reasons for shutting down blockchain mining in China.[23] Energy consumption was also cited in a Russian central bank proposal to ban bitcoin mining (Reuters.com 2022).

Bitcoin Mining Income

Bitcoin and many subsequent DLT systems are based on a global network of independent miners that operate processing facilities that record transactions in the blockchain. Miners earn income in two ways – creating new coins that are credited to their accounts and earning fees for processing transactions.

Creating new coins. Miners compete to solve a very difficult mathematical computation; the winner is awarded a number of newly created bitcoins. In 2023, 6.25 bitcoins were awarded for each iteration of the process, which occurs about every 10 minutes. In early 2024, the award is expected to be halved to 3.125 bitcoins per iteration. Because a reward is made only to the first miner with the solution, miners often form pools to increase chances of gaining a reward which is then shared

---

[23] The restrictions resulted in an initial sharp drop in processing in China, which prompted major shifts in mining into Kazakhstan, the United States, and elsewhere. However, after the sharp decline bitcoin mining has partially recovered.

between pool members. Large groups have formed to the point that mining is dominated by only a handful of groups.

Processing fees. In a typical situation, a customer approaches an exchange to handle a bitcoin transaction. The exchange announces to miners the transaction to be processed along with information about the fee the customer is willing to pay.

Based on the length of the transaction (measured in terms of bytes of data) and the fee offered, miners decide whether they will accept it. Fees reflect the number of coins offered per byte processed, which must be sufficient to cover miners' variable costs, which is usually mostly electricity.

Fees also vary because of the limited processing capacity of the system. In 2021, an average ten-minute session handled just over one million bytes of data. If capacity is reached, miners accept transactions offering the highest fees first; those with lower fees are processed later or ignored.

Fees rise at periods of high demand or when system capacity is stretched – for example, very sharp spikes in fees occurred around year-end 2018, in mid-2021, and early 2023. The possibility that the system cannot handle panic demand and thus will generate fee spikes is a clear threat to the soundness of the system.

In summary, bitcoin processing can be slow with volatile fees which is unacceptable for many retail transactions, but might be efficient for larger financial transactions, such as for international payments through correspondent banks.

The general public does not transact directly within the bitcoin system. The public can buy or sell bitcoins at 'exchanges' that price the value of the bitcoins in terms of the official national currency and charge fees for their services. The national currency price of a bitcoin can differ between exchanges.

Customers' bitcoin holdings are held in "wallets" that record the owner and the amount held. (The wallet lists the number of coins – not the value of the coins in the official national currency).[24] The current market value of the coins on an exchange determines the value of the coins in the wallet.

Satoshi Immortalized

Fractional pieces of bitcoin are needed for many purposes; for example, to handle small commercial transactions or pay small processing fees to bitcoin miners. The standard fractional unit of bitcoin (BTC) is called 'Satoshi' equal to a 100-millionth of a bitcoin, or satoshi = .000,000,01 BTC.

A satoshi has a market value based on the local currency BTC price. In a real-world example; at 10:27 pm UTC April 22, 2023, the BTC price was US$27,563.80. (Data are from bitcoinfees.earn.com, 2023) Thus, the equivalent satoshi price = (2756380¢ × .000,000,01) ≅ .0276¢ per satoshi). (The term satoshi applies only to bitcoin; other coins use different terms.)

Altcoins and Stablecoins

Altcoins

The pathbreaking bitcoin framework quickly fostered many different crypto instruments, often referred to as "altcoins" (alternative coins). Most altcoins change various features of the bitcoin model to enhance speed, usefulness, marketability, or provide additional functions. Also,

---

[24] The holder (or the exchange) must retain a record of the coins held – if that record is lost (including by the exchange or theft from the exchange) any value from the coin is permanently lost – the same as if cash were destroyed. A significant number of bitcoins are believed to be permanently lost.

"native coins" or "utility coins" were designed for exclusive use within specific or proprietary payment systems or to serve specific clients.[25] By mid-2021, the global total value of altcoins began to rise above the total market value of bitcoin. Because altcoins are embedded in many specific financial niches, they will continue to exist in some form regardless of what might happen to bitcoin. The diversity of altcoin experiments complicates their treatment as economic instruments, which can affect accounting, tax treatment, supervisory oversight, policy action, and analysis. Many altcoins have failed, but thousands still exist.[26]

Customers, businesses, and regulators will need to follow developing altcoins and international guidance on their treatment. A comprehensive regulatory framework over all forms of digital instruments is the ideal[27]

---

[25] Among the thousands of altcoins, Ethereum stands out as the second most used. It has two major differences from bitcoin; (1) it is programmable which makes it useful for many business purposes thus generating real demand for it, and (2) in contrast to the bitcoin 'proof-of-work' method to verify transactions, Ethereum is transitioning to the 'proof-of-stake' method which is much more energy efficient.

[26] Bitcoin dominated the crypto market during the first dozen years. Altcoins began slowly but many appeared beginning around 2017 and during the bitcoin price spike in 2021. Over time, altcoins – with more advanced features, less energy consumption, better consumer protection, or better governance features – might overtake bitcoin in general usage or become lead instruments within some market segments or for certain functions.

Two largely parallel markets have developed – one for the original bitcoin and entities directly derived from it, and the second focused on altcoins and their use for general business purposes. Although daily price movements between bitcoin and the leading altcoins are often closely correlated, bitcoins and altcoins probably should be analyzed separately.

[27] Chapter 4 describes European Union efforts to create a comprehensive framework over digital assets. The model there probably defines best current international practice over crypto instruments and deserves to be widely followed.

but their diversity makes this challenging – including the observed tendency for some altcoins to be designed to avoid regulatory oversight.

Stablecoins

Stablecoins are an important type of altcoin linked to the value of a currency, currency basket, or basket of noncurrency assets (commodities such as gold, securities, derivatives, etc.). The first stablecoin, which was linked to the U.S. dollar, was issued in 2014; it remained fairly inactive until bitcoin began to rise in value in 2017, at which time many new stablecoins were created.

Stablecoins have value based on the reserves or collateral that back them.[28] Stablecoins linked to a single currency can be exchanged for that currency and must have ready backing in that currency. Stablecoins linked to a currency basket will vary in value with changes in the value or composition of the currencies in the basket.[29]

Single-currency stablecoins reflect the value and returns of the underlying currency, but have no direct link with central bank money or formal banking institutions. An example might be a mobile phone company creating its own single-currency digital coin to facilitate transactions by its

---

[28] The nature of the reserves and the stablecoin's holder claim on them is important. Does a stablecoin holder have a claim on the firm offering the stablecoin, or can the holder claim the underlying asset? What rights exist over proprietary reserves or digital assets used as reserves? What rules govern financial collateral in specific countries? What rules govern stablecoins issued or reserves held in foreign countries? These are not simple questions to answer, but have become increasingly important during 'crypto winter' as some stablecoins have fallen below their stated values or have failed entirely.

[29] The multicurrency basket behind the ECU (European Currency Unit that preceded the euro) demonstrates properties of multicurrency stablecoins. (Krueger 2022)

customers with each other.[30] On a wholesale basis, a single-currency stablecoin could facilitate international transactions, settle interbank balances, temporarily park assets outside of the formal banking system or outside regular operating hours, or handle transactions within closed proprietary systems.

A multicurrency stablecoin could be relevant in several situations. For example, had the technology existed prior to the founding of the European Monetary Union, a multicurrency stablecoin constructed as a weighted measure of the participating currencies could have been used instead of the European Currency Unit (ECU), the virtual currency that preceded the introduction of the physical euro. Future currency unions could explore creating a multicurrency stablecoin as a step toward creating their new union currency.[31] As another example, a stablecoin could be matched to the IMF's Special Drawing Rights (SDR) basket of currencies.[32] Stablecoins for other regional groupings of currencies (GCC or ASEAN, for example) might be developed.

The type, extent, and liquidity of the reserves used to back stablecoins is critically important – a stablecoin can be judged by its reserves

---

[30] This example might be relevant as a means to enhance financial inclusion – mobile phone systems in developing countries have increasingly provided basic banking services to customers otherwise without easy access to banks and other formal banking institutions. For example, phone-based transactions can be conducted with customers in different cities that were previously impossible using cash. A proprietary stablecoin might be used in lieu of using banking facilities – but it would have many economic and policy implications.

[31] For example, in 2023 Argentina and Brazil announced exploration of a new currency arrangement to facilitate mutual trade with the possibility of creating an officially-operated stablecoin or CBDC.

[32] Many issues arise in constructing a basket: currency weights, changes in exchange rates, trading bands, portfolio 'hardening', interest returns and remuneration of holders of the basket, among others. Krueger (2022) discusses many of these issues that arose in the operation of the ECU currency basket.

backing and can be subject to the same risks as its reserves.[33] Reserves of stablecoins could include other stablecoins, other cryptoassets, or instruments correlated with bitcoin or other altcoin prices. Under crisis conditions, demands for stablecoins' reserves could correspond to declines in the value of the reserves, thus transmitting financial stresses between coins or creating market instability.[34]

Also, some stablecoins back their coins using mathematical algorithms that adjust multiple reserve assets to statistically provide full backing for the coin. The reserves might include digital assets, which individually can be volatile, and thus supervisors and the public can be unclear about the quality of reserves. This was highlighted by problems beginning in 2022 involving several arbitrage-based algorithmic stablecoins (CNBC.com 2022a).

Smart contracts and DeFi

Smart Contracts

Many altcoins build upon the flexibility of the blockchain to create new applications or append programs to the chain. Thousands of variations have been created.

---

[33] Similar issues arise for central bank reserves and commercial bank capital. Commercial banks are therefore subject to stringent capital adequacy standards and might have access to official backup liquidity and swap facilities. Stablecoins, in contrast, are largely unregulated, lack transparency, and lack the backup protections available to the formal institutions.

[34] Reflecting potentially high volatility in the value of cryptoassets held by banks as reserves, the Basel Committee on Banking Supervision (2022) set very high capital requirements for bank holdings of such assets. CBDCs avoid this issue because they are fixed-price central bank liabilities, and banks holding the CBDCs can be supported by central bank emergency lines of credit.

'Ponzinomics'

It is often asserted that many cryptoinstruments are 'Ponzi' schemes.[35] Some are clearly fraudulent or poorly designed, but others are not. It can be difficult to evaluate even legitimate cryptoinstruments because their returns can be volatile and they can have opaque finances, accounting standards, reserves, etc. and often are not subject to official supervision. A key concern is the amount and quality of reserves behind schemes – with emphasis on cryptoassets using other cryptoassets or algorithms as reserves.

Given the long string of failed cryptoasset schemes, general advice must be to thoroughly investigate first and not invest more than you can lose. A good rule is do not borrow to invest in cryptoassets.

CBDCs, as official liabilities of central banks, are intended to overcome the risks and frauds that might accompany private cryptoassets.

An important feature is the ability to program "smart contracts" or applications ("apps") into the system that automatically document and execute transactions as conditions are met or take alternative actions if conditions are not met. Smart contracts can initiate transactions with full finality when conditions are met and record the transaction in the blockchain.[36] Other actions are possible, such as transferring ownership rights, releasing collateral on completion of a transaction, or charging a sales tax on applicable store purchases. Multiple smart contracts can be built

---

[35] Charles Ponzi was a U.S. thief who sold fake investment instruments offering very high returns. To build the reputation of his offerings, he paid dividends to early investors out of receipts from later investors, which worked until the supply of new investors dried up. He was arrested in 1920 for mail fraud.

[36] For example, a contract could pay the difference between the market price of oil – on a specified market and time – and a strike price, which is equivalent to a financial future. The smart contracts are embedded in the blockchain, establish a permanent record, and cannot be changed. Likewise, records of the market events that initiate transactions are also embedded into the blockchain.

into a digital instrument to create complex financial instruments, create derivative-like instruments, customize altcoins, create proprietary systems for individual firms or industries, or handle special market conditions.[37][38]

BIS General Manager Agustín Carstens (2023) has said that the ability to use smart contracts and record their conditions and obligations into a public block chain can open up many important financial innovations. He cites a role for 'tokenized deposits', which would be regular deposits at banks recorded as tokens on a blockchain; such deposits could be efficiently used in payment systems because of their backing by central bank reserves or CBDCs.

---

[37] Consumer protection aspects of smart contracts are very important because transactions can be initiated automatically with full finality. A phrase sometimes applied to such contracts is "Code is Law" which implies that programmed smart contracts can either provide firm guarantees in a positive sense or harmful actions without recourse in the case of poorly constructed or fraudulent contracts.

A danger is that contracts can be agreed and enforced without involving lawyers and legal or regulatory oversight. They have been described as "unregulated investment funds," which of course should attract supervisory scrutiny. Building oversight and remediation systems over smart contracts will be a thorny problem for future regulators. (The EU's Markets in Crypto-Assets (MiCA) Regulation (See Chapter 4) addresses these concerns). Rigidities in such systems were shown in fall 2021 when a programming error mistakenly sent $162 million in tokens to depositors' accounts. The protocol could not retrieve the funds and recipients were asked to voluntarily return funds less a 10% reward for their honesty (CNBC.com 2021).

[38] Hypothetically, countries could take advantage of the existing technical skills of commercial digital platforms to create their CBDCs (or alternatively a parallel regulated stablecoin linked to the national currency). The instruments could use smart contracts to customize to individual country needs and use a blockchain to verify and settle transactions and monitor activity for policy and supervisory purposes. This option could allow countries to contract for CBDCs quickly and efficiently, but could outpace legal and institutional preparations.

In effect, apps or smart contracts can be embedded in altcoins for use in transactions processed on a blockchain. Securities, commodities, or real assets could be represented in an easily transferable form similar to standard financial assets. This can reduce costs and can be done independent of banks and official financial infrastructure.

Hard Forks and Kill Switches

In 2016, the Ethereum altcoin, which was designed to support smart contracts, was hacked resulting in theft of about $50 million in its ether coin. To recover the funds, the system administrators decided to roll the entire network back to the day before the hack, add a software change that excluded the hack and restored the funds, then rerun the system. The full community then had to choose whether to use the new software or retain the original version, which was referred to as a 'hard fork' in the road. The new version was adopted.

The decision was controversial – the retroactive fork modified the ostensibly unchangeable smart contract that had been settled and recorded in the Ethereum blockchain. Also, the changeover was made by the Ethereum community without involvement of regular legal dispute mechanisms, but was justified as resolving a serious problem and protecting users' assets.[39]

As of March 2023, these issues are part of EU legislation that would require provisions to allow users to stop or reset smart contracts, which were referred to as "kill switches." But in the words of a law professor, "It endangers smart contracts to an extent that no one can predict." (Schickler 2023)

---

[39] In 2017, bitcoin effectively experienced a fork when its processing code was used to create an alternative coin 'bitcoin cash' that increased bitcoin's 1 megabyte (1 million bytes) block size to up to 32 MB. The larger blocks can cut congestion, increase throughput of transactions, and lower transactions costs.

Decentralized Finance (DeFi)

The term "decentralized finance" or "DeFi" is used to describe techniques that effectively emulate bank lending or other formal financial activities. The full complement of cryptomethods (coins, stablecoins, DLT, smart contracts, etc.) can be used to carry out conventional financial activities (lending, securities, derivatives, financial transactions, settlement, etc.) without working through banks or other regulated financial institutions.[40] Numerous DeFi schemes with many different features have been created – creating regulatory, legal, and policy challenges.

Because DeFi can operate outside the regulated financial system, the rights, obligations, and legal certainty associated with DeFi operations are unclear and might not be covered in existing regulatory and legal frameworks. Accounting and statistical reporting of DeFi positions and risks might be incomplete or nonexistent. Also, monetary policy control could be affected and banks and existing financial institutions might be destabilized if financial activity shifts to unregulated channels.[41]

Libra

Libra was proposed in 2019 as a stablecoin backed by a multicurrency basket to directly compete with the central bank monetary system. Libra was to be rapid, inexpensive, inclusive, and capable of handling the very large volume of transactions that occur globally each second.[42]

---

[40] For example, a DeFi system might use a proprietary stablecoins for all internal transactions, but use a currency-denominated stablecoin to interface with the general public to handle cross-border payments transactions.

[41] During 'crypto winter' many DeFi systems collapsed with major losses to investors. In order to survive the crisis, some systems introduced voting systems for depositors to allow changes to the arrangements.

[42] IMF (2020) covered Libra and similar coins as 'GSCs – Global Stablecoins' and reviewed their international financial implications. The monetary and legal status of GSCs was found to be unclear, and although they can have monetary

(continued)

27

Libra was designed as a digital coin for use by a consortium of banks, payment systems, credit card companies, computer and mobile phone operations, and other financial businesses that interact with the public and then conduct settlements between themselves using Libra within a permissioned distributed ledger system. Libra was to be backed by multicurrency reserves contributed by consortium members. The responsibilities of meeting financial regulatory rules would remain with the individual members of the consortium.

Libra was quickly and strongly criticized by numerous central banks and finance ministries.[43] The Finance Minister of France said that Libra would not be allowed to become a sovereign currency that could threaten countries' monetary sovereignty and raises serious risks in the areas of consumer protection, privacy of customer's finances, money laundering, and financing of terrorism (Munster 2019). The U.S. Federal Reserve Board said it had serious concerns about Libra's impacts on money laundering, consumer protection, and financial stability (Barber 2019). The U.S. President's Working Group on Financial Markets (2021) has also cited potential concentration of power due to stablecoins, such as Libra.

The ECB Crypto-Assets Task Force (2020) thoroughly reviewed implications of Libra-like stablecoins as an 'alternative store of value' on monetary policy, financial stability, and financial and payment infrastructure; amongst positive features the Task Force also found a broad range of problems and disruptions.

---

policy implications, as unofficial instruments they would not be official units legally. Diverse national classifications of GSCs (money, e-money, securities, commodities, or undefined under existing statutes, etc.) could seriously complicate cross-border settlement of transactions and legal resolution of claims.

[43] The international financial community (IMF, BIS, G20, etc.) began investigating cryptoassets prior to the first bitcoin price spike in 2017, but the announcement of Libra raised the imminent possibility of a private digital currency and quickly spurred widespread action and public statements about official plans.

The Task Force also considered a scenario for issuing

> "CBDCs with technical and functional features similar to stablecoins, making their value proposition redundant at least for domestic payments and delivering the highest level of stability for users in a monetary jurisdiction." (p. 18)

The sharp criticisms quickly forced changes in the proposal. The concept of a multicurrency stablecoin was dropped in favor of single-currency backed coins, the name was changed to Diem, and issuance deferred until regulators' concerns are resolved.

The Libra announcement had two immediate effects – central banks accelerated work on CBDCs and to strengthen the regulatory regime over cryptoassets. Dealing with stablecoins will be an important project that countries will need to monitor. International bodies are quite active working on how individual countries and regional bodies should handle cryptoassets. Given the global reach of cryptoassets and official skepticism about stablecoins, coordinated international standards and actions are likely.

Chapter 3. CBDC Pioneers

The first public CBDC projects began in 2019. As potential guidance for other countries, this section reviews several projects and notes their priorities, innovations, and sometimes problems. Work since then has proceeded very rapidly. (Boar and Wehrli 2021)

In contrast to what might be expected, the pioneers are not the United States and the other major monetary center economies. Small- or low- and middle-income economies have been among the first to launch rCBDC projects to serve their citizens that lack access to affordable and convenient financial services. Providing financial services to small businesses, large young populations, women, and minorities are key motivations in many of these countries. China is the major player in this story as it seeks to provide services to very large swaths of its economy and also promote the yuan as a potential competitor to the U.S. dollar.

In contrast, major money center economies (Japan, Euroarea, United Kingdom, United States, etc.) and emerging economies (Brazil, India, Indonesia, Saudi Arabia, and others) are approaching CBDCs cautiously to better understand the consequences before leaping and to avoid disrupting already effective private payments systems.

Eastern Caribbean Currency Union: DCash

In early 2019, the Eastern Caribbean Currency Union (ECCU)[44] introduced a pilot project called 'DCash', a CBDC that trades at par with the ECCU dollar (EC$).[45]

---

[44] The ECCU comprises Anguilla, Antigua and Barbuda, Dominica, Grenada, Montserrat, St. Kitts and Nevis, St. Lucia, and St. Vincent and the Grenadines. The Eastern Caribbean dollar is pegged at EC$2.70 to the U.S. dollar.

[45] As a cash equivalent, DCash has a fixed value to the EC$ and cannot pay interest. However, instantaneous rollover into banking accounts might be

(continued)

The program is part of an overall strategy to increase use of electronic payments throughout the union, with increased use of debit and credit cards and DCash substituting for cash and checks. Specific problems DCash addresses are high costs of payments and banking services, inadequate banking services for some customers, and slow settlement of checking transactions – especially inter-island transactions. DCash was adopted gradually by different jurisdictions beginning in March 2021. In January 2022 a technical problem shut the system down for two months until system upgrades were made (ECCB 2022).

DCash is distributed through financial institutions and authorized agents. Financial institutions handle the usual documentation requirements for customers to receive regulated financial services.[46] These customers are given "register-based" wallets that have flexible ceilings for holdings of DCash based on customers' individual profiles. In addition, an effort to include users without accounts at financial institutions allows them to obtain "value-based wallets" from authorized agents (such as mobile phone operators). Transactions using these wallets are limited to EC$2,700 (US$1,000) per month.

Customers load their wallets by trading in physical cash or transferring funds from existing bank accounts. Balances in wallets can be converted back to cash or credited to accounts at financial institutions.

The central bank transfers DCash upon request to financial institutions and service providers, but total issuance is subject to a limit.

---

feasible; thus, excess funds in wallets might be swept daily into interest-bearing bank accounts.

[46] These requirements include "know your customer" (KYC), anti-money laundering (AML), and countering the financing of terrorism (CFT) rules, and other national rules such as for tax reporting.

Mobile phone service providers will provide digital wallets to store DCash and handle customer transactions. Records maintained by the providers might permit restitution of funds if wallets are lost.

Example: Market purchase using DCash

Amy goes to Bertha's Fabric store to purchase material to make a dress. Amy has a DCash wallet on her mobile phone. She selects her fabric and buttons and pays for them using the QR code on Bertha's mobile phone. She types in the amount of the purchase, authenticates it using her password, then completes the transaction.[47] The transaction is instantaneous, with DCash immediately taken from Amy's wallet and put into Bertha's wallet. A record is created on both Amy's and Bertha's wallets.

The transaction is equivalent to Amy using cash Eastern Caribbean dollars to purchase the fabric from Bertha.

Transactions between customers and bank and service providers, while not fully anonymous, are likely to be confidential at about the same level as bank transactions. Confidentiality rules might be strengthened by additional regulations. While person-to-person transactions might have more confidentiality than those involving institutions, they are unlikely to be as completely anonymous as cash.

The pilot program operates using a business-oriented blockchain platform based on a DLT platform. Unlike the original bitcoin-type platform that involves global access to an encoded blockchain, the ECCU system limits access only to processors granted permission. The system has the flexibility to add or adjust features, such as limiting the size or types of transactions, holding funds in escrow, and accommodating smart contracts. The platform can also track and reverse transactions.

---

[47] A QR code is a square image, readable by a mobile phone app or camera, containing a barcode of information. The QR code can quickly convey information about a party in a transaction.

The project has moved to a second phase involving DCash use for government payments to the public and several enhancements to improve public experience – more public education efforts, increased wallet security, and adding notes to transactions to facilitate record keeping and reconciliation between users and merchants. Such enhancements deserve consideration by other CBDC issuers.

The 2020 IMF Article IV consultation (2020) with the ECCB noted advantages and risks of the DCash plan and argued it should proceed cautiously. Advantages could include reducing excessive reliance on cash and cheques, improving efficiency of the retail payment system, and supporting economic development by reducing financial frictions. Among safeguards cited were the limited size of holdings and transaction values, no interest accruals, and exclusion of foreign currency transactions. However, it could expose the ECCB and the financial system to risks such as financial disintermediation and cybersecurity risks. Updating legal and regulatory frameworks was seen as needed. (IMF 2020b pp. 47-48)

An Article IV update in 2022 suggested dividing operational, oversight, and risk management responsibilities between the central bank and the technology providers, and establishing a project management governance framework. ECCB authorities reported that cybersecurity was the main risk with DCash (2022a, p. 26).

To summarize, the DCash pilot project provides a working example of how other systems might be developed.[48] The process is clearly complex and could challenge the resources of smaller countries or those with weaker legal/regulatory systems.

---

[48] The developer of DCash was also chosen for Nigeria's CBDC, called eNaira, issued in late October 2021.

The Bahamas: Sand Dollar

In October 2020, The Bahamas launched the Sand Dollar, a digital version of the Bahamian dollar, pegged to the U.S. dollar. The official website (sanddollar.bs) cites advantages as (1) providing faster, more efficient, and secure payment services, (2) enhancing financial inclusion in the country's small islands, (3) providing nondiscriminatory access to payment systems, and (4) defending against money laundering, counterfeiting, and other illicit activity.

Residents can integrate their Sand Dollar holdings with existing bank accounts. Visiting nonresidents are subject to limits on holdings and monthly transactions. External transactions continue to be handled through commercial banks, thus maintaining central bank controls.

As of early 2023, take up of the Sand Dollar has been limited due partly to fewer visitors during the Covid pandemic and evidently confusion between the Sand Dollar and private cryptoassets issued by an exchange based in the Bahamas. The failure of the exchange also probably increased public uncertainly about the CBDC.

Cambodia: Project Bakong

Cambodia recognizes the U.S. dollar as a medium of exchange alongside its own currency, the riel. In 2020, the National Bank of Cambodia launched Project Bakong, a quasi-CBDC system that links a DLT system with existing bank accounts and mobile phone wallets to provide inclusive retail payments in either currency. The public loads Bakong wallets with riel or U.S. dollars, then makes payments using QR codes that are cleared within the system and verified using a permissioned DLT platform designed by a Japanese company. Transactions are quick, interbank fees are low, and customer transactions are free. Due diligence and other supervisory tasks remain with the member financial institutions.

Project Bakong is explicitly intended to reduce the use of U.S. dollars; with the project launch, the National Bank of Cambodia ceased distribution of U.S. $1, $2, and $5 banknotes.

The project began slowly, with 1.4 million Bakong transactions and about 6 million uses of on-line apps linked to the system during the first half of 2021 (Takemiya 2021), then showed more rapid growth beginning in 2022 (Phnompenpost.com 2022). If it continues to operate successfully and becomes more popular, its dual-currency feature could become an important model for other countries to follow.

Laos and other Southeast Asia and Pacific Islands

Influenced by Project Bakong and with Japan government assistance, Laos[49], Vietnam, and several Pacific Islands countries (Fiji, Solomon Islands, Tonga, and Vanuatu) are investigating CDBCs. All are using the company operating Project Bakong. (Atlantic Council 2023)

Laos is undertaking a proof-of-concept exercise to create a CBDC called DLak. Because around 70% of Laotians do not have bank accounts (Khmer Times 2023), they would use a remote device such as a mobile phone. Banks would purchase DLak from the central bank using cash then exchange it with customers using fiat currency and place it on the customers' device. Customers and merchants can immediately exchange it with each other or at banks for cash, thus avoiding sometimes quite lengthy settlement times. A key factor might be whether banks interacting with customers maintain sufficient cash liquidity to be able to exchange DLak for cash on demand.[50] DLak could be a promising model for a number of countries with large populations with limited or no access to bank services.

---

[49] Laos is receiving assistance from the Japan International Co-operation Agency – JICA. (Ma 2021).

[50] This problem occurred at times in the e M-Pesa phone operated transactions system in Kenya when local venders did not carry enough cash to redeem customers' credits.

China: E-yuan (e-CNY)

Beginning in 2021, China gradually introduced a retail digital currency through a pilot project. It began as pilot projects in several cities and by mid-year had reached about 10 million users. There are ambitious plans for the e-CNY, including creating a cross-border rCBDC for the 'Greater Bay Area' (Guangdong-Hong Kong-Macao). (PBOC 2021)

The e-CNY is issued through the banking system. Payments can be made using smartphones via QR code connections and online. At this time, it is intended for domestic retail use with access for visitors; existing payment systems continue for international transactions. Processing is centralized rather than DLT.

The e-CNY is programmable and can initiate transactions when preset conditions are met. This is seen as assisting fiscal and monetary policies and monitoring cross-border transactions. (Eckberg and Ho 2021)

Official encouragement to use the e-CNY has led to several regional pilot projects – Changshu city has decided to pay its employees in e-CNY, the Hong Kong Monetary Authority intends to work with the People's Bank of China to explore use of the e-CNY for cross-border payments within the region (Ma 2023), and Xuzhou, as a major international railroad shipping center, is promoting use of the e-CNY in 'Belt and Road' countries to pay for trade services. (Feng 2023).

Internationally, China seems to be promoting greater use of the yuan for settlement of overseas transactions and for denominating oil contracts. The e-CNY could facilitate these trends.

Given the size of the Chinese economy and its strong economic ties to Southeast and Central Asia and elsewhere, the e-CNY has potential to become a major international reserves and transactions instrument.

Despite the creation of several hundred million e-CNY accounts, the actual use is still quite limited – data from the People's Bank of China for end-December 2022 showed that the e-CNY comprised only 0.13% of narrow money (M0) (Coindesk.com 2023). Contributing to the slow usage were probably the slow-down of the economy due to the Covid epidemic and existing good access of urban populations to convenient payment systems. Despite the slow start, its ability to compete against private payments systems and to reach enormous rural populations will be closely watched and could provide important lessons for other countries.

Concurrently with its official promotion of the e-CNY, China's central bank sharply restricted private crypto operations. In 2021, private cryptocoin mining operations were forbidden, as were many crypto exchange services. A deputy governor of the central bank said that the private coins had fostered destabilizing speculation and facilitated illegal activity and money laundering, and that stablecoins could affect international payment and settlement systems (Bloomberg News 2021).

Nigeria: eNaira

Nigeria launched an eNaira demonstration project in October 2021 with a contract with the same firm that issued the ECCB's DCash. Nigeria is Africa's biggest economy and its CBDC could have widespread influence, but the project has started slowly and neither the public nor merchants have shown much enthusiasm (Cointelegraph 2023b).

Perhaps partly in response, the central bank in January 2023 published *Payments System Vision 2025* (Central Bank of Nigeria 2023) to review the national payments system. It looks to apply best international practices to reflect and regulate new payments methods, including CBDCs and a wide range of other digital innovations (stablecoins, blockchain applications, distributed finance, cyber security, smart contracts, artificial intelligence, etc.). A regulatory environment would be developed that would foster innovation, including considering the regulatory regime needed to issue "Initial Coin Offerings" (ICOs) that are treated as a "novel" digital asset class issued like a security to raise capital or fund lending (Cointelegraph 2023a).

El Salvador Bitcoin Experiment

CBDCs, bitcoin, and stablecoins are potential competitors as monetary instruments. In mid-2021, El Salvador declared bitcoin as legal tender. Because El Salvador is fully dollarized and does not issue its own currency, its recognition of bitcoin gives El Salvador two legal currencies. Recognition of bitcoin was advertised as promoting greater financial inclusion and reducing the cost of remittances into the country.[51]

The law introducing bitcoin as legal tender required all businesses to accept it unless they lacked the technology. To encourage use, El Salvador created a wallet called Chivo that instantly converts bitcoins into U.S. dollars. Transactions using Chivo are intended to be commission free. Each Chivo was preloaded with $30 worth of bitcoins as an incentive to join, which led to a surge in sign-ups for the system. ATMs to load Chivo wallets were installed and arrangements were made with bank branches to load or use Chivo.

The experience thus far has not been good, with complaints of fraud, insecure wallets, and violations of know-your-customer (KYC) rules.[52] Very few bitcoin transactions are made for remittances or purchases and many Chivo wallets are not used or used only for U.S. dollar transactions (restofworld.org 2022). An international ratings firm said that holding bitcoin would probably be a negative factor in insurers' ratings because of its volatility, accounting and legal uncertainties, and additional costs

---

[51] The regional development bank, the Central American Bank for Economic Integration (CABEI), reportedly was interested in whether bitcoin can cut the cost of sending remittances and thus assisted in drafting a legal framework for bitcoin as a currency.

[52] Fluctuations in bitcoin prices while undertaking a transaction caused some unfortunate arbitrage opportunities that some customers could exploit.

involved. Overall, the decision was described as "unnecessarily rushed" (Decentralized.trading 2021).[53]

In January 2022, the IMF Board advised El Salvador to remove bitcoin as legal currency, and a survey in March 2022 found that it was little used in transactions (Bloomberg 2022a, 2022b).

The project continues and many adjustments have been made to deal with problems (Pymnts.com 2021). It remains to be seen whether the country's rushed and incomplete preparations spell the demise of bitcoin as legal tender in El Salvador. Importantly, it provided a real-world demonstration that bitcoin might not perform well as a transactions currency.

Bank of Botswana Warnings on Cryptoassets

In November 2021, the Bank of Botswana issued a public warning about some consumer protection problems that can arise (Bank of Botswana 2021).

- There is no prevailing legal or regulatory framework for cryptoassets and customer are at complete risk.
- It is prudent to investigate the registration and legality of entities offering cryptoassets as well as their sources of income.
- Some cryptoassets activities are similar to pyramid schemes and scams that could cause participants to unwittingly participate in criminal activity and expose themselves to legal risk and loss.
- 'Cryptocurrency' is a misnomer because cryptoassets lack the fundamental characteristics of currency.
- Other than the existing general bank legal framework, "the public would have no recourse to the Bank of Botswana for redress

---

[53] See Krueger (2022, chapter 3) for a discussion of legal concerns associated with parallel currencies.

pertaining to fraud, misconduct, or financial losses emanating from or associated with participation in the crypto assets business."

- The Bank of Botswana recognizes that effects of cryptoassets on financial markets and mandates could be pervasive and significant, and thus continuing monitoring is needed.

Unfortunately, this statement probably reflects the situation regarding cryptoassets in many countries – a solid legal framework is still needed over all private cryptoassets and the general public must be educated on their characteristics and risks. Work to issue CBDCs and integrate them into the economy would be additional separate efforts.

Other Countries

As of May 2023, the Atlantic Council (2023) listed 114 countries issuing or investigating CBDCs. Chapter 4 has a case study on a future digital euro. Other large countries working on CBDCs include Japan, UK, and US, and an effort by the BRICS countries (Brazil, India, Russia, Saudi Arabia, and South Africa)[54] to investigate CBDCs as part of an effort to create a non-US dollar payments system. rCBDCs are the main focus in 47 countries; 21 countries are working on both rCBDCs and wCBDCs; 8 countries are focused on wCBDCs. The rest are undecided.

Most of the larger countries appear to be approaching CDBCs cautiously, such as on a 3-to-5-year schedule. In part this reflects adequacy and public acceptance of existing payment systems. It can also reflect that introduction of CBDCs will be complex and can revolutionize (or potentially disrupt) financial markets. It also appears that the larger

---

[54] India has a limited pilot program for both wholesale and retail digital rupees. Russia signed legislation in late July 2023 to create a CBDC, reportedly in part to work around sanctions and to further trade with China. Saudi Arabia participated in Project Aber, one of the first explorations of CBDCs and has continued research. South Africa has a pilot wCBDC program and in Project Dunbar is participating with several other countries investigating using CBDCS in cross-border transactions.

countries are placing more emphasis on use of CBDCs to facilitate international transactions.

Among medium- and small-sized economies, emphasis is placed on rCBDCs to promote financial inclusion, modernizing domestic financial systems, and reducing remittances costs and delays.

IMF Handbook on CBDCs

In response to requests from its membership, in Spring 2023 the IMF described how it would support the building the countries' capacity to investigate and implement CBDCs.[55]

Requests for IMF assistance are broadly based, roughly equally spread between Africa, Asia, the Middle East and Central Asia, and the Western Hemisphere. Few requests have come from Europe, reflecting the work already underway there by the ECB and European Union.

Demand for assistance is such that the IMF says it will need to prioritize assistance to systemically important countries and to countries that are fast-tracking CBDC development and have capacity constraints and weak regulatory systems.

---

[55] IMF Approach to Central Bank Digital Currency Capacity Development. IMF Staff Report Policy Paper 2023/016. April 10, 2023.

Chapter 4. Case Study: The Digital Euro[56]

This chapter covers the digital euro and its surrounding EU framework. Chapter 5 covers some similar international CBDC initiatives. Together, these projects are creating the rules, standards, and systems that will drive most countries' future CBDC endevours.

The work in Europe to create a digital euro CBDC is the best available large-scale example of how a fully configured CBDC system might operate. The digital euro model is fully cognizant that it will exist surrounded by private cryptomarkets and thus a comprehensive framework covering all types of digital assets is needed. At this time, the digital euro model provides the best available model to guide CBDC work by other countries and regions.

Although the digital euro is not yet issued, work on it and the surrounding legal and supervisory frameworks is advanced and well documented. The model addresses the full institutional, policy, and legal/regulatory aspects of digital finance, including how private digital instruments fit into the picture. Gaining familiarity with the work in Europe is a good starting place for almost any student – and indeed for any country seeking to create their own CBDC.

A digital euro would revolutionize the European monetary picture, with global consequences.[57] It would meet demands for efficient, inclusive instruments to support the European economy and facilitate cross-border

---

[56] See https://www.ecb.europa.eu/paym/digital_euro/html/index.en.htm. An update is expected in October 2023.

[57] In March 2022, U.S. President Biden issued an executive order requiring government agencies to investigate crypto markets, including possible development of a U.S. dollar CBDC and consider policies promoting investor protection, financial stability, and prevention of illegal use of cryptoassets. In a February 2023 paper, the Bank of England and HM Treasury (2023) declared that a retail digital pound would be needed and listed some likely features. A report by the Group of Central Banks (2020) (see Chapter 7) is also noteworthy.

transactions. It would facilitate further integration of the Euroarea financial system by allowing rapid low-cost financial transactions and transmission of monetary policy impulses across the region.[58] It also would change market dynamics, require new institutional and legal arrangements, and raise new types of risks.

The Cash Euro[59]

It can be argued that creating a digital euro is as complex as creating the original cash euro. All the concerns and steps involved in creating cash carry over into the digital realm, but new issues arise. *A priori*, it is suggested that anything involved with cash also applies to digital.

The cash euro is produced up to the highest global levels of quality and usefulness. It took nine years to move from the initial Working Group on Printing and Issuing a European Banknote to its ultimate circulation in 2003. The process was deliberative and inclusive to produce money that would symbolize the unity of the new Europe and provide maximum protection against counterfeiting.

Euro bills and coins moved smoothly across the new monetary union and were designed to facilitate use by the public, money handlers, vending machines, ATMs, and money processing machines. Strict standards

---

[58] The 1992 Maastricht Treaty, which founded the Euroarea and the euro, envisioned a single fully integrated financial market between countries using the euro. A digital euro would facilitate that goal. Importantly, because the Euroarea is a part of the European Union, which provides an overarching framework of laws and institutions, a digital euro would be obligated to further advance the EU's democratic and economic programs. In turn, EU laws, directives, and judicial rulings have facilitated the use and success of the euro – later in this note several EU-level actions are described that directly support a digital euro and regulate private cryptoassets. These EU actions should be treated as integral parts of the digital euro model.

[59] Rösl and Seitz (2022) review recent euro cash supply and demand. They note a "cash paradox" in Europe in which cash use at point-of-sale (POS) has decreased although total issuance of cash euros has increased.

were put into place to ensure circulating money was clean and undamaged – damaged money was promptly withdrawn from circulation.

The cash euro quickly became the most widely circulating currency in the world and has lived up to its expectations. But its use, like that of physical currency elsewhere, has steadily declined as the public switches to electronic forms of payment.

The possibility of electronic money ('e-money') was recognized from the launch of the cash euro. A 1998 report to the European Commission (EMI 1998) concluded that e-money could significantly affect monetary policy and seigniorage. Thus, rules governing its issuance were needed and were enacted in an EU framework for "electronic money institutions" (EU 2000). The framework absorbed e-money firms into the ECB's monetary financial institutions (MFI) framework that covers firms that handle cash and monetary deposits and loans – thus, cash money firms and electronic money firms broadly fall within the same policy/regulatory framework.

Producing a digital euro CBDC will be at least as challenging as producing the cash euro – there is no reason to think a digital euro can be produced any easier or faster than its cash predecessor.

In 2020, an ECB Report (ECB 2020) cited advantages of creating a digital euro and possible implementation strategies:

- Support digitalization of the European economy to promote productive innovation and efficient payment systems. A digital euro can help support interoperational payment systems throughout the union, thus advancing integration within the union.[60]

---

[60] Digital payment systems within the union are supported by a 2014 EU Regulation that established standards for electronic IDs and signatures. This ancillary legislation will be needed elsewhere.

- Deal with the significant drop in the use of physical cash that could undermine the sustainability of cash services in the union. A digital euro would help guarantee public access to riskless public money.
- Counter possible deep penetration of the European economy by other countries' CBDCs or private digital instruments (such as stablecoins). Competitors could affect monetary transmission, create foreign exchange risks and exposures, and affect retail channels.
- Support monetary policy options, including the possibility of remunerating the digital euro to reflect policy interest rates.
- Exploit the ability to build resilience and back-up capabilities into the digital euro to mitigate dangers of cyberattacks, natural disasters, power cuts, or shocks that could affect other systems.
- Support the international role of the euro. The report suggests this could involve cooperation with other central banks to create interoperable systems between CBDCs (See Chapter 6); such systems could reduce international payments frictions without giving nonresidents direct access to the digital euro.
- Improve the cost structure and ecological footprint of monetary and payment systems.

The next pages describe the ECB report, which provides a useful model for others' work on CBDCs. The process is clearly complex and lengthy with multiple consequential decisions needed along the path.

Market Impacts of a Digital Euro

The report looked at the market impacts of a digital euro and how it could affect official monetary and payments functions in Europe. Some impacts were expected to vary depending on whether the public directly holds digital euros or whether they are intermediated by banks and other financial institutions.

The report reviewed the possibility of financial instability because of disintermediation if the public shifts deposits away from banks into safe digital euros.[61] In particular, the public could shift into the digital euro very quickly, which might increase both the likelihood and severity of bank runs.[62]

The digital euro could also affect the central bank balance sheet, income, and role within the broader financial structure. The possible impacts on the central bank cited in the report included the following:

- substitution of the digital euro for cash
- a net change in central bank liabilities
- whether the CBDC will be remunerated
- loss of seigniorage
- types of access (if any) by nonresidents
- the type, extent, and liquidity of the central bank's assets (including official reserve assets) held against the digital euro liabilities
- the possibility of banks needing loans from the central bank as a result of losing deposits.

According to the paper, costs of issuing a digital euro need to be considered – how will new infrastructure and operating expenses be covered? Will fees be charged? Can seigniorage cover the costs? Will the entire system or specific parts of the system be subsidized? Also, the central bank might gain responsibilities, costs, and risks of operating a retail

---

[61] Such shifts might be accelerated during periods of negative interest rates on deposit accounts if the digital euro is like cash with a fixed 0% interest return. Analyses of possible deposit-to-CBDC shifts have all shown some effect, but size estimates vary. Gross and Letizia (2023) developed a model that can show very little to near complete substitution of CBDCs for cash depending on the parameters and amount of remuneration offered on the CBDC.

[62] In the face of deposit withdrawals, banks could compensate by raising their offered rates, borrowing from capital markets, or borrowing liquidity from the central bank (which would require banks to hold collateral against their liability to the central bank).

payment system, including constructing failsafe systems to handle emergencies.[63]

International exposures of the digital euro could vary depending on whether rCBDC or wCBDC systems are set up and if any restrictions are placed on international transactions and exposures. The report says possible digital euro cocirculation outside the Euroarea could unsettle the exchange rates, markets, and 'monetary sovereignty' of those countries.[64]

'Monetary Sovereignty'

Internationally, the digital euro will change Europe's international monetary and payment arrangements to take advantage of its efficiency and

---

[63] The report says relatively little about financial inclusion, likely because Europe is already well endowed with smoothly operating financial institutions serving the public. In contrast, in many countries, promoting financial inclusion is a key motivation for an rCBDC, but this involves creating new systems for small-scale transactions or serve populations that are uneconomic for existing banks to handle. Building in standardization of procedures and interoperability of systems will be critical. If the ECB chooses to issue an rCBDC, it would need to investigate the many aspects of its use by the public.

In an rCBDC system, existing institutions could be affected or new institutions and payment patterns might be needed. A variety of new legal arrangements might be needed to facilitate new payments arrangements and settle the rights and obligations of the parties involved.

[64] Currency substitution effects within potential regional unions might inhibit union development if a regionally dominant country's CBDC spreads throughout the region and suppresses options for the union to create its own CBDC. For example, the eNaira might become competitive throughout much of Africa. Staunching such international digital currency substitution suggests creating m-CBDC Bridge systems (see next chapter) that use defined channels between separate countries' CBDC systems.

cross-border flexibility. But it (and other large country CBDCs) might also penetrate and threaten smaller national currency markets.

In economics literature, 'monetary sovereignty' is considered the right of a nation state to issue its own currency and exercise its own monetary policy. The penetration of a financial system by outside currencies goes by various names – dollarization, cocirculation, currency substitution, etc. Country efforts to defend their national financial markets from penetration by alien currencies, private stablecoins, and CBCDs is referred to as defending 'monetary sovereignty'. [65]

Creating one's own CBDC backed up by appropriate legal shields is a partial defense against alien CBDC penetration, but might be overwhelmed by factors such as the economic strength of large neighboring countries or convenience in using foreign CBDCs in trade transactions.

"The right to issue and control digital currencies will become a 'new battlefield' of competition between sovereign states." per an article in China Finance cited in New York Times (Popper and Li 2021). A plausible response for economically smaller countries and regions might be to collaborate on regional CBDC-based payment regimes or accelerate work on monetary unions.

The report says that placing conditions on use outside the Euroarea would be useful to avoid volatility in flows and exchange rates. Decisions will also be needed on any remuneration of nonresident holdings and any sharing of seigniorage. Holdings outside the Euroarea might also facilitate criminal activity.

---

[65] Harold, Landau, and Brunnermeier (2019) say "The best defense against digital dollarization may be for countries to issue their own currencies in digital form by creating central bank digital currencies (CBDCs). CBDCs are hotly debated from the perspective of monetary policy and financial stability. However, they may have a more fundamental justification: to adapt domestic currencies to the new state of technology and, in the process, to protect them from outside competition based on digital superiority."

A final concern is to build in the highest levels of resilience and redundancy to withstand shocks, protect data, and recover values if needed.

Legal Considerations

The report describes some legal implications of creating a digital euro and guaranteeing its use as legal tender. Legal implications of four distinct uses for the digital euro were reviewed with the conclusion that *each type of use would employ a different legal backing*:

- It might be used only as a monetary policy instrument with central bank counterparties.
- It could be a settlement instrument between eligible counterparties.
- It could be available to Euroarea residents through accounts held with the Eurosystem.
- It could be equivalent to a banknote available without restriction.

The report states that, "Retail access of the digital euro entails considerable legal novelty." Moreover, some options would involve private distributors, which would require legal arrangements for private entities integrated with official rules and regulatory procedures.

Designing the legal system for the digital euro will be complex given existing rules, multiple system options, diverse public and private actors, different country legal arrangements, multiple European market supervisory institutions, and levels of legislative action. It is apt to be even more complex in future unions whose legal frameworks are less unified than in Europe.

Design Considerations

A retail digital euro of course would be available online or when connected to a mobile phone or other telecommunications, but also needs to be available when customers are not connected, that is offline. Swipe cards, chips on handheld devices, point-of-sale (POS) scanners, etc. will be needed to allow CBDCs to be part of regular daily activities. Online and offline versions of a retail digital euro probably should be issued simultaneously, and their respective designs must be compatible.

An important aspect is user privacy. Unlike cash, the report states that existing rules do not permit anonymous digital transactions, and full anonymity might not be possible.[66] Also, systems that involve private entities need strict rules on access to and use of private information.

Limiting Holdings of the Digital Euro

In addition to limiting holdings to slow disintermediation from existing financial institutions, the ECB specifically raises the issue of how a digital euro would interact with the negative interest rate monetary policy.[67] This concern is now outdated.

Channels for Cross-Border Flows

Noting the serious risks from unrestricted international use of the digital euro, the report calls for investigation of an approach in which countries

---

[66] Among official reasons for limited anonymity are possible restrictions on holdings by nonresidents, limits on large transactions, tracing for criminal investigations, as well as for KYC, AML, and CFT reasons.

[67] If the digital euro is unremunerated like cash, "It does not seem feasible under current circumstances to offer unlimited holdings of digital euro to corporate entities at zero interest rates" because unrestricted access would disrupt monetary policy.

More relevant is whether digital euros should have limits on holdings and transactions similar to what has been suggested for the cash euro. The idea of limiting holdings of cash euros is not new. To deter money laundering, corruption, financing of terrorism, etc., several Euroarea countries have limits on euro *cash* transactions and consideration has been given to creating an EU-wide limit (perhaps €10,000) on cash transactions.

establish supervised channels between separately operated CBDCs.[68] This allows any two countries to maintain their monetary and exchange rate policies while permitting international flows that can be monitored in case compensatory actions are necessary.

Accounting and Verification

The digital euro system needs a mechanism to ensure that only legitimate instruments are transferred and that transactions are credited to the right parties. The *cash* euro imbeds many features to prevent counterfeiting and permit private cash processors to verify authenticity (Krueger 2022, chapter 9). The report says, "a similar level of security in the digital environment with multiple sources of cyber risk *is much more complex, and this risk is not yet fully understood*" (p. 25, emphasis added).

The report discusses account-based systems in which transactions are verified by the central bank, by private supervised entities, or bearer systems. In bearer systems, responsibility to verify transactions rests with the two parties involved; in a potential modification of the bearer system, the report suggests that payment devices in the Euroarea might include built-in restrictions on certain transactions. Moreover, it suggested that the central bank could limit payment devices to only entitled users, which would require such users to confirm their identities.

Some Conclusions of the ECB Report

The report has a highly ambitious program to
- design a system,
- educate the public,
- set up supporting infrastructure,
- design policy instruments,
- introduce the legal framework,
- set up accounting and statistical systems,

---

[68] Such as the m-CBDC Bridge and Project Aurum approaches described in Chapter 6.

- coordinate with private entities,
- negotiate international arrangements, and
- allocate resources and implement the full system.

The report usefully presents the types of issues that should be reviewed by other countries in planning for CBDCs. *The program has a scale and complexity similar to the original launch of the European Monetary Union and the euro two decades ago. Countries will need to be well prepared for the road ahead.*

Two-Year Digital Euro Test

The proposed system was complex and needed testing. In late 2020, the Eurosystem began a series of experiments to test the key aspects of possible systems and conducted a large-scale survey of public views. The investigation covered four main areas: creating a digital euro ledger, privacy and anti-money laundering defenses, limiting euros in circulation, and facilitating inclusiveness and users' off-line access.

In July 2021, the ECB announced that test results had been favorable and no technical problems were found.[69] The "throughput" (processing speeds and volumes) of its in-house payments system TARGET and blockchain technology were tested and both were found to be able to process 40,000 transactions per second.[70]

---

[69] The TARGET system was found to consume negligible amounts of energy compared to DLT bitcoin processing.

[70] The excellent throughput of TARGET resulted from a two-decade long evolution to create a unified, rapid, and efficient payments system. The original TARGET system for monetary policy operations and interbank euro transactions was built upon national payment systems because of lack of time to build a new system before launch of the union. In 2007-08, a centralized TARGET2 (T2) system was created to provide real time gross settlement (RTGS) payments between banks using central bank money. In 2017-8, TARGET2-Securities (T2S) was created to harmonize securities transactions across the Euroarea. T2S

(continued)

Based on the positive results, the ECB launched a two-year "digital euro project" to design a prototype technical system, consider how to distribute the digital euro, consult with user communities and industry groups, interact with legislators, consider how to adapt the EU legal framework, examine market impacts, and more. Following these investigations (ending around fall 2023), a decision can be made whether to proceed to launch the digital euro.

This book considers the Eurosystem's preparations for a CBDC as a model for CBDC work in other countries and regions. The development of the digital euro has grown organically as a part of the monetary and financial integration processes in the Euroarea and the European Union. The euro model as it might be applied in other countries and regions encompasses the digital euro as (1) a monetary instrument, (2) a payments instrument, and, crucially, (3) as part of the overarching European

---

supports rapid delivery of securities upon payment (DvP) of central bank money with full settlement finality.

In 2018, the Eurosystem augmented its TARGET payment scheme with a mechanism for rapid processing and settlement of transactions called TARGET Instant Payment Settlement (TIPS). It was designed to permit instant payments between bank accounts anywhere within the Euroarea.

In TIPS, banks place reserves into an account at their national central bank that can be used for settling transactions instantly using central bank money. A bank sends a payment order to the TIPS system, which validates the order and then transfers funds to the receiving bank. Transactions usually are sent and settled within 10 seconds. TIPS transactions are very cheap, fast, and available 24 hours a day.

TIPS was also designed to be scalable to meet demand. The ECB tests in late 2020 showed that it could also handle a large volume of digital euro transactions. Successful tests were also made using a blockchain system. The tests showed that the TIPS system is highly efficient and competitive with any new digital system.

Union financial sector infrastructure and supervisory/legal framework that supports it.

The digital euro in the European Union Framework

In designing the digital euro, the ECB is an institution within the overarching European Union framework. As such, it is obligated to reflect EU goals and follow EU rules. Major actions at the EU level thus affect the digital euro but also financial markets in additional countries.[71]

Foundations of EU E-Money Regulations

Prior to work on CBDCs, the EU had a legal framework covering electronic money. Elements of the framework were originally found in an ECB report (1998) that set minimum requirements for e-money systems that remain highly relevant today;

- Issuers of electronic money must be subject to prudential supervision.
- Issuance must be subject to sound and transparent legal arrangements.
- Technical security must be assured, including the ability to detect counterfeits.
- Protection against criminal abuse is needed.
- Monetary statistics reporting is required and companies must supply information needed for monetary policy purposes.
- Issuers of electronic money must be legally obliged upon request to redeem electronic money against central bank money at par.

---

[71] The legislation described in this section applies to all European Union member countries, not just those countries that have officially adopted the euro. In May 2023, the EU comprised 27 countries, but only 20 "euro area" countries use the euro as their official currency. The digital euro will be official money of the euro area countries, but other EU countries retain their own currencies. However, all 27 countries follow EU regulations related to e-money, digital assets, and payment systems, etc.

- Central banks can impose reserve requirements on all issuers of electronic money.
- Electronic money systems should be interoperable.
- Insurance, loss-sharing schemes, or guarantees are needed to protect the holders of electronic money.

The requirements meant that electronic money could operate as a single market linked with the official monetary market (cash and bank money), which avoided the possibility of the market operating with different liquidity or risk conditions from the overall market or between systems. Interoperability between all systems would widen consumer options, reduce users' costs, increase competition, encourage innovation, and allow switching between services.

Digital Operational Resilience Act (DORA)

This Act enacted in 2022, effective in 2025, bolsters the robustness of information and telecommunications infrastructure of the European financial sector to prevent serious disruptions to operations. Digital service providers are explicitly placed under regulatory control of financial sector supervisors. EU-wide standards are proposed to prevent divergences between national efforts. Authorities gain power to request information, conduct inspections, issue risk management rules, and issue recommendations subject to fines for failure to comply.

Importantly, it *forbids European financial firms from using infrastructure not located in the EU but which is critical for operations within the EU.* For example, a major data processing facility in Hong Kong would not be permitted to operate bank operations in Italy. Another important step is setting up a common reporting arrangement for reporting infrastructure failures or attacks.

Markets in Crypto-Assets Regulation (MiCA)

The European Union ratified MiCA in April 2023. It is the first regulation to comprehensively regulate cryptomarkets. Regulations for stablecoins (which are an area of heightened concern) are effective after 1 year, but other provisions become effective over 18 months.

MiCA is designed to bolster innovation and competitiveness in the EU financial system by supporting initiatives in digital finance and protecting against the new risks involved.

The EU found that the existing financial services rules did not cover most cryptoassets and could inhibit instruments based on DLT. Also, regulation was fragmented by legislation enacted by individual countries. The EU concluded that a common framework was needed to address such concerns, provide consumer protections, strengthen market resilience, and build larger and more competitive crypto markets.

Priorities in MiCA are:

- Provide legal certainty for all forms of crypto-assets in a common EU framework,[72]
- Support financial innovation,
- Provide consumer and investor protections,
- Maintain financial stability,
- Address environmental concerns, and
- Provide "Safeguards to address potential risks to financial stability and orderly monetary policy that could arise from stablecoins."

MiCA notes that the "structure of stablecoins is complex and comprises many interdependent functions and legal entities." Thus, it seeks to "create a comprehensive and holistic EU framework on stablecoins, capable of mitigating the risks identified … in particular financial stability risks."

---

[72] The agreement focuses on crypto-asset firms and exchanges. Bitcoin is not covered (because it is not issued by a firm) and crypto-asset mining is not prohibited. NFTs (nonfungible tokens) are not covered, but the EU Commission was mandated to investigate whether regulations are needed.

MiCA states regulations should be proportionate to their need and risks addressed. It "imposes more stringent requirements on 'stablecoins', which are more likely to grow quickly in scale and possibly result in higher levels of risk to investors, counterparties, and the financial system."[73]

The strategy for stablecoins calls for legislation (largely based on FSB recommendations) that addresses stablecoins' risks[74] and extends the preexisting EU Electric Money Directive to cover stablecoins because they have many characteristics of e-money, are stores of value, and can be used for payments. Placing stablecoins under the E-money umbrella also helps prevent arbitrage between the conventional and digital regulatory regimes. Reserves were required to cover mass withdrawals and daily limits placed on transactions.

MiCA is an integral part of the EU model with direct effects on CBDCs and potential competitor digital assets. It might provide guidance to other countries and regions seeking standards for crypto-assets markets and how they should be regulated.[75] Analysis of the market and institutional impacts after MiCA is implemented in 2024 could provide valuable information to other countries on how their cash and banking markets could be affected.

---

[73] MiCA. Section 2. Legal Basis, Subsidiarity, and Proportionality.

[74] Parallel to the FSB concept of Globally Systemically Important Financial Institutions (G-SIFIs), the term 'global stablecoin' foreshadows the possibility that stablecoins might become systemically important within the global financial system and become risks to global financial stability, and thus would require special oversight. A concern about stablecoins is that substantial links between a stablecoin and banks could destabilize banks if a stablecoin fails. MiCA partly addresses this concern by putting a €200 million cap on stablecoin transactions per day by individual banks. (Digitalpoundfoundation.com 2023)

[75] An important feature to limit misuse of crypto-assets is to require reporting of transfers over €1000 between crypto exchanges and individual wallets.

Pilot Regime for Market Infrastructures based on Distributed Ledger Technology (DLT)

Given the complexities and rapid changes in cryptomarkets, the EU enacted a Regulation in May 2022 that lays out an evolutionary process in which actions to support innovations in the market (while adhering to the MiCA priorities and protections) as new financial practices develop and experience is gained in market oversight.

The project focuses on three market innovations; cryptoassets, the "tokenization" of traditional financial assets, and use of DLT in financial services. Financial assets are broadly redefined to include digital financial instruments based on DLT, crypto-assets not covered by existing EU financial regulations, and e-money tokens.

The project mandates that all European Supervisory Authorities[76] review how their regulations apply to cryptoassets, identify areas for improvement, and consider strategies to make their frameworks friendly for innovation.

It was recognized that some existing rules would inhibit development of DLT instruments[77] – especially those requiring centralized registry of financial instruments and activities that clash with the decentralized transacting and recording under DLT. The pilot regime seeks to overcome such obstacles: With a common EU pilot regime for the experimentation of DLT market infrastructures, firms could exploit the full potential of the existing framework, allowing supervisors and legislators

---

[76] European Banking Authority (EBA), European Securities and Markets Authority (ESMA), and European Insurance and Occupational Pensions Authority (EIOPA).

[77] "Existing financial services legislation was not designed with DLT and cryptoassets in mind. This means that there are provisions in it which sometimes restricts and even prevents the use of DLT."

to identify obstacles in the regulation, while regulators and firms themselves gain valuable knowledge about using DLT.

The regime allows supervisors flexibility "to determine which provisions to disregard for a market participant's test to allow different test cases. The pilot regime will enable regulators to remove regulatory constraints that can inhibit the development of DLT market infrastructures, which could enable the transition to tokenised[78] financial instruments and DLT market infrastructures, enabling innovation and ensuring EU's global competitiveness."[79]

The regime requires harmonized requirements to issue cryptoassets or obtain authorization to provide services for cryptoassets. It would also harmonize operational and disclosure requirements for service providers. These steps would allow firms to operate across the single market which should increase their efficiency, reduce complexity of instruments and operations, simplify burdens for consumers, and provide better and simpler consumer and investor protections.

To summarize, the EU regulations above seek to lever the innovative features of the new financial technology while addressing the broad range of risks and protections associated with cryptoassets – consumer protection, investor protection, legal finality of transactions, money laundering, criminal activity, financial stability, and monetary policy implications.

The EU regulations are an integral part of its model covering the multifaceted aspects of the new digital technologies – communications,

---

[78] "Token" might be defined as an encoded message that stands for something else. In this case, it might refer to a blockchain-tradable version of an underlying financial instrument. Thus, a "tokenized deposit" would be a bank deposit that has been recorded digitally as a token that can be transacted in interbank digital payment systems.

[79] Prudential Regime. Sect. 2. Legal Basis, Subsidiarity, and Proportionality.

storing value, transacting, making payments, and settling positions. Each aspect must operate efficiently and securely to support the European economy and its growth, provide customer protection, facilitate monetary policy action, and maintain financial soundness.[80]

Digitalization and its diverse and interrelated impacts are global phenomena – other countries often will need to take steps to reform their financial systems similar to the actions being introduced in Europe.

---

[80] The European Systemic Risk Board has described how high levels of "interconnectedness across financial entities, financial markets and financial market infrastructures, and particularly the interdependencies of their ICT systems, might constitute a systemic vulnerability since localized cyber incidents could quickly spread". ESRB (2020)

Chapter 5. International Initiatives on Digital Assets

In addition to the work underway in the EU, international organizations and standards setting bodies (SSBs) are advancing work relevant to CBDCs. Several important initiatives are covered below. 2023 has seen a burst of public reports that highlight the breadth and intensity of work that had previously been largely undertaken internally. The first two reports below summarize work investigating CBDCs and global standards for regulating cryptoassets.

<u>BIS (Bank for International Settlements) Innovation Hubs</u>

BIS Innovation Hubs are set in multiple regions to investigate and develop policy related to technological innovations, such as CBDCs, Artificial Intelligence (AI), cybersecurity, DLT, etc.[81] The Hong Kong Hub is working on Project Aurum reviewing the interactions between wCBDCs and rCBDCs. The next chapter covers CBDCs and cross-border transactions, such as Singapore Hub work on a multicurrency 'm-CBDC Bridge' and the Nordic Hub's Project Icebreaker (which is focused on a cross-border rCBDC platform). The various projects are gaining important information about CBDC operations and are helping setting international standards for such systems.

Project Aurum was the BIS Innovation Hub's first rCBDC project. It has a domestic economy focus, linking a wholesale interbank system and a retail system. (Project Aurum[82] 2022) (Other Innovation Hub

---

[81] It must be noted that *at this point* these investigations do not commit to any particular payments technology, such as DLT. Existing payments systems in many countries have instant payments systems (IPS) that appear capable of handling CBDCs, which might make countries hesitant to commit to DLT.

[82] Project Aurum is run by the BIS Innovation Hub in Hong Kong and the Hong Kong Monetary Authority. The source code for the system has been made available to other central banks to help support CBDC development elsewhere.

projects dealing with cross-border transactions are covered in the next chapter.)

Project Aurum integrates a wholesale interbank CBDC issued by the central bank with retail stablecoin wallets backed by CBDCs within the banking system. The stablecoins are liabilities of the issuing bank backed by assets held by the central bank, which partially blurs the distinction between CBDCs and stablecoins. The system leverages the existing financial system infrastructure used by the public and businesses and allows financial firms to innovate services to the public.[83]

BIS Report 'Lessons learnt on CBDCs'

In July 2023, the BIS submitted a report to the G20 Finance Ministers and Central Bank Governors on results of the various CBDC 'proof of concept' projects it has sponsored during the previous three years. The next chapter describes some cross-border CBDC projects to enhance cross-border payments. Several projects (Hong Kong, Switzerland, and UK) focus on domestic CBDC use and in particular Project Polaris supports financial inclusion by producing a large handbook on how CBDCs can be used off-line to serve many rural or isolated populations, operate in areas with poor on-line connections, or in emergencies.

The report notes that all early circulating rCBDCs notes have been adopted slowly, and there are concerns about privacy and

---

[83] The Project Aurum paper (2022) discusses intermediated CBDCs and the degree of 'decoupling' between the underlying CBDC offered by the central bank and the retail instrument offered to the public. A complex tradeoff is involved, affecting the central bank operational burdens, market innovations, interoperability between bank systems, decoupling of wholesale and retail ledgers, cyber security, confidentiality of user information, and bank supervision, etc.. These concerns must be addressed in line with national financial and legal conditions. These considerations make it possible that a wide variety of national solutions might be forthcoming.

legal/regulatory situations. For cross-border uses, two models have been used – a shared common platform (m-Bridge) or hub-and-spoke model (Icebreaker). Both models were found useful – the hub-and-spoke model was found easier to implement, but the shared platform is capable of more intense development.

Governance of CBDC systems is seen as a challenge, especially for cross-border systems that deal with multiple legal, institutional, and regulatory frameworks.[84]

FSB Global Regulatory Framework for Crypto-Asset Activities

In mid-July 2023, acting on a request by the G20 (Group of 20), the FSB (Financial Stability Board) published recommendations to create comprehensive and globally consistent regulations covering cryptoassets and global stablecoins. CBDCs are not subject to the regulations.

The Framework is based on the principle of 'same activity, same risk, same regulation". (The financial press reported the report meant that cryptofirms would 'have nowhere to hide'.) The report notes that cryptoassets are intrinsically volatile and can transmit financial stresses throughout the financial system. The report focuses on risks to financial stability, proposing actions proportionate to the risk involved, but seeks to do so in ways that support digital innovation.

An annex lists specific activities to address, with separate major sections on cryptoassets and stablecoins because of their different financial risk and policy implications.

---

[84] As described in Chapter 4, in Europe the overarching EU legal framework considerably facilitates potential CBDC issuance by erasing many governance, legal, and institutional differences between countries. Elsewhere, further development of regional currency unions could also help support CBDC issuance and governance. Or perhaps regions might elevate the harmonization of cross-border payments as a priority in their regional financial integration efforts.

The FSB has coordinated with IMF investigations of macroeconomic and policy implications of cryptoassets, with a joint report to the G20 scheduled for September 2023. The FSB, IMF, and SSBs have prepared a shared workplan with tasks and schedules running into 2025.

The Framework does not cover CBDCs, but changes to the crypto regulatory universe will affect how CBDCs will be designed and operate. Also, the recommendations for stablecoins could be relevant for CBDCs because they might compete with each other and some distinctions between the instruments in use or public perception could blur.

G20 Roadmap for Enhancing Cross-border Payments

In 2020, the G20 countries launched a major initiative to upgrade international payments. Acting along with the FSB, it created a comprehensive 'Roadmap' of actions to improve cross-border payments (lowering costs, speeding transactions, improving access, improving security, etc.) by creating common standards, involving both public and private sector participants, improving transparency, and coordinating regulatory and legal frameworks. (FSB 2022)

The Roadmap covers many aspects of cross-border payments extending well beyond CBDCs. Nineteen explicit recommendations, with follow-up arrangements, were developed with CBDCs explicitly covered only in number 19. As the Roadmap is implemented broad changes in international financial arrangements will occur that will affect how CBDCs will be designed and operate – in principle, the Roadmap will smooth the introduction of CBDCs. And market integration of CBDCs with private cryptoassets will probably also be eased.

Roadmap building blocks perhaps most relevant directly or indirectly to CBDCs are;
- #4 Aligning regulatory, supervisory, and oversight frameworks for cross-border payments,
- #5 Applying AML/CFT rules consistently and comprehensively,
- #8 Fostering KYC and identity information sharing,

- #11 Exploring reciprocal liquidity arrangements across central banks (called 'liquidity bridges'),
- #14 Adopting Harmonized ISO 20022 for message formats (see text box below),
- #17 Consider the feasibility of new multilateral platforms and arrangements for cross-border payments,
- #18 Foster the soundness of global stablecoin arrangements for cross-border payments, and ….
- #19 *Factor an international dimension into CBDC design.* (This point is the focus of Chapter 6, below.)

The Roadmap in its entirety is setting global standards – CBDCs in their role as payment instruments will need to be compatible with it.

BCBS Standard on Banks' Prudential Treatment of Cryptoassets

In December 2022, the BCBS (Basel Committee on Banking Supervision) issued "Prudential Treatment of Cryptoasset Exposures" that provides a useful split between two types of cryptoassets based on their risk treatment within bank capital (BCBS 2022):

- Group 1: Assets that can be classified under regular BCBS capital standards, and

- Group 2: All the rest that will face more stringent standards. Banks are not permitted to hold more than 2% of Tier 1 capital in these assets, and strong capital reserve and liquidity requirements are imposed.

In light of the inherent price risk of bitcoin, it (and similar cryptoassets[85]) is classified in Group 2 and receives a punitive risk weight of 1,250% on bank holdings of bitcoin, which means (when multiplied by the 8% required capital ratio) that the bank must hold regulatory capital equal to 100% of its bitcoin holdings.

---

[85] The punitive risk weight also applies to any private cryptoasset that does not meet a set of strict standards laid out in BCBS (2021).

The formulas below (as shown in BCBS 2021) show that banks must hold capital equal to the value of bitcoin holdings. This is equivalent to saying that banks must hold enough capital to write-off the full value of their holdings (that is, the value of bitcoin falls to zero).

Bank holdings of bitcoin x 1,250% = Risk weighted assets (RWA)
100   x 1,250% = 1,250

RWA x Minimum regulatory capital requirement (8%) = capital required
1,250   x 8% = 100

Moreover, a new additional capital charge covers 'infrastructure risk' to cover any observed weaknesses in underlying arrangements used for the cryptoassets.

A test for redemption risk is also introduced for stablecoins to ensure they are regulated in ways that help ensure redemption. During crypto winter, a number of cryptofirms in difficulty suspended redemptions of their coins and sometimes attempted to convert deposited assets into equity positions.

Given these restrictions and especially the low limit on permissible Group 2 holdings, it seems that bank holdings of cryptoassets might give limited direct competition to CBDCs held by banks, which is an important financial soundness result. Because own-country CBDCs will be a Group 1 asset, banks holding CBDCs will be given the most favorable capital standards permitted for central bank liabilities.

The obvious problem is that the standard applies only to banks. The EU's MiCA Regulation appears to cover the nonbank portions well, but the story elsewhere is unclear.

IMF Initiatives

As the international body tasked to maintain the soundness of the international financial system, the IMF is actively investigating CBDCs and their consequences. It is also providing technical support to countries working on CBDCs and is preparing a Handbook on CBDCs (see description in Chapter 3) to help guide countries' work in the field.

In late June 2023, the IMF announced it is working on a global platform for cross-border payments for tokenized bank holdings of central bank reserves that can be extended to CBDCs. (Adrian 2023) It is covered in Chapter 6.

IOSCO Recommendations for Crypto Assets

The IOSCO (International Organization of Securities Commissions) (IOSCO 2023) put out for public comment recommendations on trading in crypto assets, stablecoins, and relevant tokens. The *'Overarching Recommendation Addressed to All Regulators'* says investor protection and market integrity in cryptoasset markets are the "same as, or consistent with, those required in traditional financial markets in order to facilitate a level-playing field between cryptoassets and traditional financial markets and help reduce regulatory arbitrage". (p. 4) Especially important is greater consistency between countries in cryptoassets' regulation and oversight given that they fall under multiple regulatory regimes due to their cross-border trading.

An interesting aspect of the recommendations is guidance on treating vertical integration in crypto-asset platforms, either within a single firm or affiliated group of firms. Some crypto platforms create a cryptoasset and also perform trading, brokerage, custody, market-making, proprietary trading, and settlement. There could be multiple conflicts of interest within a single firm, including mixing of customer funds with the firm's. (Berwick and Wilson 2023).

ISO Standard Identification Codes for Digital Assets and CBDCs

In 2022, the ISO (International Organization for Standardization) issued ISO 20022 that included a standard for 'Digital Token Identifiers' (DTIs) that identify digital assets in international financial messages.

Cryptoassets must meet rigorous standards in order to be accepted as ISO 20022 compliant (including putting messages into XML – eXtensible Markup Language – format) to be acceptable for international financial communications, such as central bank messaging systems and financial databases such as Visa and Mastercard. The changes help make previously incompatible payment platforms interoperable.

The new standard will facilitate use of CBDCs for international and other financial payments by providing a common language for exchange and settlement of CBDCs between countries or in domestic transactions.

The EU has adopted ISO 20022 as a further tool to reduce costs and frictions in payment systems. The United States is transitioning in 2023. In March 2023, SWIFT (Society for Worldwide Interbank Financial Telecommunications) transitioned (and upgraded) its system to handle the new identifiers and message structure with the expectation that participating banks and other financial institutions will adopt the new standard by end 2025.[86]

Digitalization and tokenization are blurring the lines

Tokenization is the digitalization of assets to allow their trading on markets. Tokenization can cover an extremely broad range of assets and could engender major changes in financial markets and institutions.

> "2022 saw a range of tokenization initiatives across the globe – reflecting the emergence of tokenization as an area of focus of the wholesale banking community." (UK Finance 2023)

---

[86] ISO 20022 covers a very broad range of financial transactions and instruments. It can be used for international payments, domestic bank transfers, securities, automated clearing houses (ACH), and more. The ISO (in ISO 6166) also gives securities (bonds, derivatives, and equities, etc.) 'International Securities Identification Numbers' (ISINs). If digital derivatives (futures, options, etc.) are ultimately assigned ISIN codes, they might become ISO 20022 compliant which would facilitate their transfer and settlement.

CBDCs can be viewed as a specific type of digital financial instrument that exist alongside an ever-broadening range of cryptoassets and tokenized assets. Markets can choose whichever instruments best fit specific purposes;

- In over 60 countries, Instant Payment Systems (IPS) already provide rapid transactions and instant settlement.[87] IPS can actively compete with CBDCs; Conversely, central banks might use CBDCs to enhance transfer and settlement within their IPS.
- Consumer banking options are well advanced in many countries which has tamped down public interest in CBDCs.
- Stablecoins might actively compete with CBDCs.
- Digital instruments might be programmable and serve diverse public or private market purposes. (CBDCs can also be programmable.)
- Tokenized bank deposits seem widely viewed as a popular choice.
- Tokenized assets can offer remuneration, usually unavailable in cash-like CBDCs.
- Tokenized government securities have been issued in some countries and could compete with CBDCs. (The European Investment Bank has tested digital bond issues.)
- Tokenization can change the liquidity and tradability of many financial assets (conventional securities, illiquid assets such as real estate, or structured finance[88]) with many diverse market impacts.

How will CBDCs relate to the situations above? Can CBDCs provide additional backing to already effective private systems? Will CBDCs destabilize the systems?

The international central banking community is well aware of critical roles of existing payments systems and capital markets that now handle

---

[87] The European Target Instant Payments System (TIPS) is cited in Chapter 4.

[88] Structured finance refers to instruments for complex financial situations that are not readily handled by conventional loans or securities. Due to its application to unique situations, structured finance is often illiquid or untradable – digitalization potentially provides liquidity to such investments.

and settle the vast majority of financial transactions. Central banks will often want to promote private digital innovation to leverage private expertise and market contacts. The roles of CBDCs in this milieu could vary country-by-country.

A discussion of the blurring and implications is beyond the scope of this book, partly because much work is still quite new and unsettled. How will blurring affect monetary policy options?[89] Students should be aware that significant changes are underway that could have major financial market and regulatory implications.

To conclude, this chapter covered major new international standards for cryptofinance and CBDCs being developed. Financial markets will be changed dramatically and soon.

---

[89] In recent decades, monetary policy analysis has often focused on 'broad money' that includes close substitutes for traditional 'narrow money' instruments. Broad money seems to give empirically better correlations with overall macroeconomic activity and prices. The blurring underway affecting CBDCs and other digital instruments likely will further broaden the boundaries of broad money to complicate statistical measurement of money and policy development.

Chapter 6. CBDC Cross-Border Projects

This chapter describes several initiatives using CBDCs for international transactions. Work in this area can perhaps be best summarized by IMF Managing Director Kristalina Georgieva at a conference in Rabat Morocco for African central banks...

> "CBDCs should not be fragmented national propositions... To have more efficient and fairer transactions, we need systems that connect countries: we need interoperability... For this reason, at the IMF, we are working on the concept of a global CBDC platform." (Bitcoinke.io 2023)

Work is underway by the IMF, the Bank for International Settlements (BIS) through its multiple regional Innovation Hubs, and multiple central banks. This chapter begins with an outline of a proposed IMF system that can handle either CBDCs or banks' tokenized reserves at their central banks in countries that do not have CBDCs. A detailed description follows of Project Icebreaker as an example of features and challenges for cross-border CBDCs systems. Several other important CBDC only projects are also described.

Watch this area closely for regularly breaking news about results of multiple investigations underway and possible new regional or global CBDC-based international payments platforms.

Project Jura

This early cross-border wCBDC project run by the BIS, Banque de France, and Swiss National Bank successfully executed real-life transactions between commercial banks in France and Switzerland. Numerous innovations in the project provided information useful in future work.

Among important innovations of the project were; transactions had to comply with current regulatory standards, certified non-resident banks were given access to the system, the system used a DLT platform operated by a third party, the wCBDC was issued on that platform, euro-denominated commercial paper was successfully tokenized, and a dual-notary sign-off procedure was used.

IMF XC Platform

The proposed IMF XC (Exchange and Contracting) Platform unveiled in mid-June 2023 is intended to be a flexible general-purpose cross-border payments system that can use either CBDCs or bank's digitalized (or tokenized) holding of central bank money. It can be used by countries without CBDCs, but can be extended to cover CBDCs or purely domestic transactions.

A first not-too-detailed description of the XC platform is as part of a "new class of cross-border and domestic payments and contracting platforms." (Adrian 2023)[90] It is seen as an important step in the evolution of money by taking advantage of technological advances in cryptography, tokenization, and programmability.[91] The XC platform seeks to create a 'trusted ledger' as a digital document representing central bank reserves tradable between system members. The key is use of central

---

[90] Adrian covers key features of the system (programmability, information management, system governance, capital flow management, implications for stability of the international monetary system, etc.) that cannot be covered here. Also, Adrian and Mancini-Griffoli (2023) have a longer paper on many of the same issues that deserves reading.

[91] The XC platform is intended to overcome much of the cost, slowness, and opaqueness of cross-border payment arrangements. Many existing systems rely on complex correspondent bank (or chain of banks) arrangements. Each bank in a transactions chain verifies identities of transactors and availability of funds which can be slow and costly. Although many improvements have been made in recent years so that transactions using well-established channels can be settled almost instantly, costly slow service still exists for those without access to the best systems and for remittances. Cross-border transactions also involve different legal and institutional arrangements between countries which complicates documentation, settlement, and dispute resolution.

bank reserves in a digital form that all parties can agree avoids counter-party risk and is instantly acceptable.

A central ledger records and settles transactions. The ledger records who owns assets and thus double-spending of an asset is impossible.

The system is explicitly designed to handle multiple currencies without creating new settlement assets. Thus, countries retain control of their monetary reserves systems and would need to make only minimal changes to existing payment systems. Complementary arrangements are needed to handle foreign currency exchange rates, manage risk, and accurately identify parties involved without unduly invading privacy

An important question is how can a centralized system with massive throughput be effectively and securely operated and governed? Who bears costs? What are rights and obligations of participants? How are disputed transactions resolved? This is obviously a massive project with many issues to resolve – keep watching this issue.

Project Icebreaker

Project Icebreaker is an rCBDC project between the central banks of Israel, Norway, and Sweden and the BIS Innovation Hub Nordic Centre. It uses a 'Hub-and-Spoke' model with a central platform that sets common rules and procedures to transact rCBDCs between countries, then permits countries to link to the hub to carry out transactions. The hub uses a common set of APIs (Application Programming Interfaces) to which different domestic systems can link. (Project Icebreaker 2023)

The hub's rules must be followed by all participating countries. Although the rules are complex to deal with diverse situations, the system is much simpler than creating separate arrangements between country pairs and dealing with their different institutional, supervisory, and legal systems. Thus, individual countries follow a single set of rules rather than potentially creating dozens of separate sets of procedures.[92]

The Icebreaker model breaks cross-border transactions into two separate domestic payments in which rCBDCs never leave their own country systems. This is achieved by separating the payment service provided by the hub from the provision of foreign exchange in the two countries

Based on the Icebreaker report, an example of a transaction might be as follows – a restaurant in Israel wants to buy sushi-grade salmon from Norway. The system arranges for the restaurant to pay in Israeli shekels and the exporter to receive Norwegian kroner.

The order is placed in the system. The hub only routes the payment message and searches for a FX provider. That is, the hub routes the message between Israel and Norway to purchase the salmon by offering kroner for it against the value of shekels used for the purchase.

The system hub searches for banks or other foreign exchange (FX) providers who maintain rCBDC wallets in both shekels and kroner. The kroner sales price of the salmon is fixed and the shekel equivalent value must be determined.

Potential FX providers submit their exchange rate offers to the hub, which selects the best rate.[93] Competition in providing foreign exchange is intended to generate competitive exchange rate offerings and provide greater market transparency and liquidity.

---

[92] Conversely, bilateral rCBDC platforms can be advantageous where a large volume of transactions occurs between two specific countries, perhaps between Sri Lanka and India for example.

[93] This arrangement that separates the hub and FX providers differs from the standard correspondent banking model in which the importer arranges payment with its own bank that both provides the foreign exchange at a exchange rate it controls and initiates the payment service.

The selected FX provider acts as an intermediary in the transaction. The FX provider incurs risk in holding the currency and managing liquidity, for which it earns income based on the spread between buy and sell rates in each currency.

The FX provider makes digital payments on a PvP (payments versus payments) basis using 'Hash Time Locked Contracts' (HTLC) that records the exact time that the contracted exchange rate is agreed. The system puts a digital lock on shekels in the payment wallet and a matching lock on kroner in the receiving wallet. When the kroner wallet recognizes that it holds the locked funds, the payments order is reviewed and if correct digital messages are sent that unlocks the kroner funds and deducts the funds from the shekel account.

Because the rCBDCs do not have counterparty risk, a competitive exchange rate can be searched and locked in, and transactions conclude at digital speeds – reportedly within a few seconds during testing.

Payments are final – the restaurant's account is immediately debited and the exporter immediately receives the funds and can use them instantly (just like cash).

In situations where limited transactions occur between two currencies, a bridge currency can be used. This is a PvPvP (payment versus payment versus payment) situation. For example, the restaurant also wants to buy cod from Iceland, but no FX provider has rCBDC wallets in both shekels and Icelandic krona. In this case, a shekel to Icelandic krona exchange rate is derived from the rate between shekel and Norwegian kroner and then between the Norwegian kroner and Icelandic krona. The use of bridge currencies gives great flexibility to the system (such as a transaction between Mauritius and Ecuador) and allows countries with less traded currencies to join the system.

Minimal requirements are needed to participate in the system; each country must have a continually operating real time (or close to real time) payments system, each must operate an HTLC system, and FX providers are available.

The scope and flexibility of the proposed Icebreaker platform show great promise. The system has an advantage that the central hub performs the bare minimum functions of (1) setting the rules to connect to the system, (2) transmitting only payments messages across borders, and (3) selecting the best available exchange rate for a transaction. The FX providers execute actual cross-border financial transactions using rCBDCs in accordance with their national financial rules and institutions.

> "Project Icebreaker shows that central banks can have almost full autonomy when designing their domestic rCBDC system while still being able to participate in a formalized interlinking arrangement to enable cross-border payments." (Project Icebreaker p. 7)

m-CBDC Bridge

This is perhaps the best known CBDC payments investigation. In early 2021, China, Hong Kong, Thailand, and the UAE (with support of the BIS Hong Kong Innovation Hub) announced a joint project ('m-CBDC Bridge') to test a multi-CBDC system for continuous multicountry cross-border foreign exchange payments-vs-payments (PvP).[94] A joint announcement said the project is intended for "central banks in Asia as well as other regions to jointly study the potential of DLT in enhancing the financial infrastructure for cross-border payments" (Hong Kong 2021).

---

[94] This form of monetary cooperation was initially investigated in the Saudi/UAE "Project Aber", which produced favorable results. Its fully documented results provide an excellent summary of how the m-CBDC Bridge could operate. (SAMA 2020).

The project is intended to address frictions, high costs, and legal and regulatory complexities of cross-border transfers, trade settlements, and capital market transactions.

The system uses a shared common platform employing DLT. A real-world experiment in 2022 involving 20 commercial banks used CBDCs issued on the m-Bridge platform by the four participating central banks. The technical transfers were successful, but revealed a range of policy and legal considerations to address regarding access of central bank money to foreigners using a shared ledger. Issues also arose regarding the fit of the CBDCs within existing country legal and regulatory frameworks. Some of the issues will involve "further development and experimentation". (Project mBridge 2022)

Project Nexus

Project Nexus uses a hub-and-spoke platform to which national instant payment systems (IPS) can connect in order to transact cross-border with other IPSs. More than 60 countries have IPSs and Project Nexus builds on that foundation in order to make international payments. With support of the BIS Innovation Hub in Singapore, in 2022 a prototype of Nexus transacted between ISPs in the Euroarea, Malaysia, and Singapore. In the current phase of work, five Southeast Asian countries (Indonesia, Malaysia, Philippines, Singapore, and Thailand) in collaboration with the Singapore Hub, are connecting their systems to the Nexus hub.

At this point the system does not use CBDCs, but CBDCs could become part of individual countries' interface with the system.

Project Mariana

This project, involving three Innovation Hubs, builds on early wCBDC investigations to examine use of wCBDCs in Automated Market Makers (AMM) for cross-border tokenized foreign exchange trading. This can be considered as application to CBDCs of concepts drawn from decentralized finance (DeFi) and an exploration of potential uniform technical standards to support interoperability of wCBDCs. (Project Mariana 2023)

Project Dunbar

This project involves the BIS Innovation Hub and the central banks of Australia, Malaysia, Singapore, and South Africa. It uses a shared multi-CBDC platform designed for direct cross-border transactions in different currencies. The platform is intended to allow direct foreign currency transactions without use of intermediary correspondent banks.

To summarize, the projects and explorations covered in this chapter present a picture of very broad investigations of CBDCs and related digital instruments, drawing on global resources and expertise. Intense research is examining the nature of the financial transformations now underway and is probing to find ways through previously unknown situations. It is an excellent example of coordinated international financial cooperation.

As successful results of these projects continue, international standards and platforms for cross-border payments linked with domestic transactions might be established in the next three to five years. The infrastructure requirements and institutional/legal frameworks can differ considerably depending on the option chosen – thus, serious diligence is needed prior to choosing the path ahead. *All countries considering CBDCs should monitor these highly promising projects and the pros and cons of each.*

Students and practicing economists will soon need to toss out a lot of existing textbooks on international payments and begin adjusting to the new infrastructure and the consequential changes in economic flows and policy.

Chapter 7. Retail CBDCs and Financial Inclusion

In May 2023, Kristalina Georgieva, IMF Managing Director, said

> "We think that wholesale CBDCs can be put in place with fairly little space for undesirable surprises, whereas retail CBDCs completely transform the financial system in a way we don't quite know what consequences it could bring."

> "I can tell you that we will see a very significant transformation that comes from CBDCs.....Now there is an engagement, and for the right reason: the future has arrived." (Strack 2023)

rCBDCs, as a secure trusted money that can be quickly exchanged and settled, can be especially important in speeding up and lowering costs of commercial transactions.

> *Under existing arrangements*, a check used by a farmer to purchase fertilizer from a local supplier will go to the supplier's bank, then be forwarded to the farmer's bank (with the possibility of additional handling by intermediary banks or a government clearing office) who will make payment after verifying that the farmer has funds to make payment. Each step incurs some costs and delays settlement of the transaction.

> *Using an rCBDC*, in contrast, can reduce or eliminate such steps – including the possibility of using mobile phones or handheld devices to make immediate payment between the farmer and the supplier. Or rCBDCs will be readily convertible into cash at banks, ATMs, or for making cash change for retail purchases.

rCBDCs will also need to be inclusively designed to ensure access to all citizens (availability in different languages, use by visually impaired, children, illiteracy, lack of internet or reliable power, lack of digital identity, etc.), and for visitors to the country.

rCBDCs can also leak in and out across borders which affects domestic monetary conditions, balance of payments flows, and potentially exchange rates and confidence in the national currency. Many countries are considering prohibiting or limiting such cross-border flows.

Another key issue is confidentiality of individual transactions. Many countries are trying to assure holders of the general confidentiality of the CBDC, but cannot grant complete anonymity (such as with cash) because of the need to defend against AML/CFT and for use in criminal proceedings. It is unclear at this point whether public concerns about confidentiality will significantly dampen acceptance of rCBDCs.

Online versus Offline rCBDCs

An online rCBDC is connected to a system that certifies authenticity, transfers value, and prevents copying and illicit reuse of the instrument. Connections could be to a central data base, bank-run systems, private systems communications systems, or DLT, etc. Connections are not always available and some populations might have limited access.

Offline systems store CBDCs on devices with computer chips (such as in mobile phones). The CBDCs can be transferred to other devices or online systems. Devices can be used remotely, whenever convenient or when online communications are unavailable, especially during emergencies. Small transactions can be made without clogging up online systems. Although offline systems are not as fully anonymous as cash, the public might find them acceptably confidential.

Disadvantages of offline systems are that they can be lost or broken, might offer no recourse for bad transactions or erased funds, might support illicit activities, transactions might not be recorded, or could facilitate cross-border flows counter to countries' balance of payments policies. Various ways exist to address these problems, but one rather common tactic is to put limits on the size of holdings or transactions.

Although both online and offline CBDCS have cash equivalents and are convertible to cash, the practical ability to convert from either to cash could be an issue, especially where cash usage has dwindled because of the popularity of CBDCs or other digital payments instruments.

Offline systems must have some kind of online connection to load up value, download into bank accounts, convert to cash, etc. These connections must be set up simultaneously with the offline system.

rCBDCs can help retain central bank control over money by countering the globally observed decline in use of cash. Conversely, cash use can be expected to continue in almost all countries and central banks will need to continue issuing cash and supporting its use, which is expensive.[95] rCBDCs will need to be designed to effectively interface with cash technically and be readily convertible into cash. Cash outlets will need to be maintained and venders of various sorts might need to hold stocks on hand.[96]

rCBDCs can also be a tool to digitize government-public financial transactions to make them more efficient, less expensive, and faster. Tasks include distributing public benefits, paying government bills, collecting taxes, etc.

IMF Financial Access Survey

The annual IMF Financial Access Survey (FAS) monitors the degree of financial inclusion and methods used. The 2022 report shows increasing use of mobile phones, especially during the COVID epidemic.

"The FAS data show a transition from traditional financial access points such as bank branches and ATMs to mobile agents and retail agent outlets in some developing economies since the onset of the

---

[95] India is reportedly promoting a digital rupee partially in order to reduce the costs of printing cash.

[96] rCBDCs can also be used as tools to reduce cash use. They can be used to reduce circulation of foreign currencies within an economy such as in Cambodia. A widely adopted rCBDC can help reduce costs of printing and handling cash.

COVID-19 pandemic. The usage of digital financial services has also increased, with the value of mobile money transactions growing from about 40 percent of GDP to 70 percent in low-income countries, and the value of internet banking transactions increasing from 225 percent of GDP to 324 percent in middle-income countries between 2019 and 2021." (IMF 2022c)

This rapid growth shows that existing payments technology – prior to the mass introduction of CBDCs – is making impressive gains in serving public financial needs. In some countries, this might dampen the urgency to develop rCBDCs or to design rCBDC systems to operate through existing payment platforms. In general, the survey results indicate that rCBDCs will coexist with mobile and digital platforms, which will affect acceptance and usage patterns on both sides of the equation.

The specifics of rCBDC systems are likely to vary greatly between countries, and possibly different payment platforms in a country will use different methods. Frictions between systems can hinder the effectiveness of rCBDCs. Interoperability between systems is a highly sought feature, which will require national rules or development of international standards.

Should Central Banks Manage rCBDCs?

Should central banks directly operate rCBDCs with the public? In some small countries, the central bank must take this role, or engage a private firm to do so. Other countries need to decide whether the central bank has the skills and staffing to do so or whether private banks are better placed to interact with the public, provide innovative financial services, and handle the burdens. Central banks might also face fears that they could destabilize financial markets or be accused of seeking to control or nationalize banking activity.

A regulatory lawyer in the U.K. has said "Any suggestion that digital money can involve direct relationship between the central bank and retail customers has the capability of causing major systemic shock and it is not clear how banks can adapt their funding models to this development." (cited by Partington 2021)

rCBDCs are complex. They are a high priority for emerging and developing economies and more complex than wCBDCs. They must serve many diverse needs, are challenging to put into place, create risks for the public and businesses, and can expose central banks to new costs and burdens.

Countries are strongly advised to implement rCBDC programs only after the points raised in the following two comprehensive lists of questions about rCBDCs have been satisfactorily answered.

List 1 – Core Attributes of rCBDC[97]

Instrument features	
Convertible	The CBDC exchanges at par with cash and bank accounts
Convenient	The CBDC should be as convenient as using cash
Accepted and Available	The CBDC should be usable in same types of transactions like cash. There must be ability to make offline transactions.
Low cost	Low cost or no cost is needed for users. Technical investments are low cost.
System features	
Secure	Users and infrastructure must be *extremely* resistant to cyber attacks. Instruments must be protected from counterfeiting.
Instant	Final settlement must be instant or near instant

---

[97] Proposed by the Group of Central Banks (2020), comprised of the ECB, the central banks of Canada, Japan, Sweden, Switzerland, United States, and United Kingdom, plus the BIS.

Resilient	The system must be *extremely* resilient to operational failure, natural disasters, and electrical outages. The system must permit off-line payments.
Available	The system should never be closed.
Throughput	The system must speedily process a very large volume of transactions.
Scalable	The system is able to expand to meet demand.
Interoperable	The system interacts with private payment systems with easy flow of funds between systems. It potentially interacts with systems in other countries.
Flexible and adaptable	The system can adapt to new instruments, new conditions, and policy changes.
Institutional features	
Robust legal framework	A central bank should have clear authority to issue a CBDC.
Standards	The system, its institutions, and participants will conform to prudential and regulatory standards equivalent to those covering firms offering cash or digital money services.

List 2 - Issues to Resolve in Creating rCBDCs

In 2021, the Monetary Authority of Singapore (2021) and several international financial organizations held a competition between developers to design a system to introduce CBDCs to the public and create the needed infrastructure. The competition included the following list of 12 issues to resolve before issuing rCBDCs.

1.   **New Functionalities vs. Inclusivity**   Can a retail CBDC system be embedded with additional functionalities beyond a basic transfer of value without requiring users to use smartphones (or other expensive/complex hardware)?

2.   **Security vs. Accessibility**   Can the design of a retail CBDC system be highly secure for users (e.g. one that prevents unauthorized uses and illicit transactions) without compromising the ease of use? Would such a system be able to cater to the varied needs of the elderly, minors, and those with disabilities?

3.   **Availability vs. Risk of Disputes**   Can offline transactions be enabled in areas with no or limited internet connectivity? What safeguards against double-spending and counterfeiting can be embedded to minimize disputes related to offline payments?

4.   **Recoverability vs. Anonymity**   In the event of theft, damage or loss of a wallet, card or instrument, can a retail CBDC system adequately trace transactions, limit the loss or support the recovery of lost funds without compromising user identity?

5.   **Widespread Frictionless Use vs. Control**   Are there technological features that can be incorporated into a retail CBDC solution to minimise the risk of significant and abrupt outflows from bank deposits to the CBDC, while ensuring that the use of the CBDC is as seamless as possible?

6.   **Personal Data Protection vs. System Integrity**   Can the retail CBDC solution protect personal and consumer transactions data, while allowing for monitoring, detection and prevention of illicit activities on the network (e.g. money laundering /terrorism financing, fraud, scams and corruption)?

7.   **Expanding Access to Financial Services vs. Guarding against Data Monopolies**   How can the design of a retail CBDC solution allow participating firms to harness payment data to enable the offering, customizing, or improving the pricing of financial services (e.g. credit, insurance) to users, while avoiding the undesirable effects of data monopolies on

consumer welfare over time? How might users retain control over use of their data?

8. **Coexistence vs. Integration Complexity** How can a retail CBDC infrastructure be made more resilient to single points of failure? Can concentration risks be minimized through decentralization? How can a safe, stable and sustainable governance model for such decentralised infrastructure with clear lines of responsibility and accountability be developed?

9. **Decentralisation vs. Accountability** How can a retail CBDC solution allow financial institutions to distribute CBDCs to the end user in a manner that leverages existing national payment rails such as a country's payment systems, while keeping participation cost competitive at minimal disruption? How can it process payments between users on different payment systems without involving additional intermediaries, or needing custom integration for onboarding?

10. **Extensibility vs. Operational Resilience** Can a retail CBDC infrastructure be flexible yet robust, allowing for computationally intensive use of programmable functions and addition of new capabilities without incurring additional overheads in terms of cost, operational performance or introducing system vulnerabilities?

11. **Privacy vs. Performance** Can a retail CBDC infrastructure incorporate privacy preserving capabilities while remaining high performing, with fast response time, low latency and scalability to support large deployment?

12. **Interoperability vs. Standardization** How can interoperability be achieved across different instruments of digital money and across different technologies without a commonly accepted standard? How can interoperability be achieved across different instruments of digital money and across different technologies without a commonly accepted standard?

Chapter 8. Digital Identity and Privacy

A very common concern is that CBDCs will allow authorities to get personal financial information. Concern about loss of privacy might affect willingness to adopt CBDCs. Privacy concerns have become a political issue, leading some to suggest CBDCs should never be issued.

In general, CBDC proposals pledge to maintain high degrees of privacy, but also note that there are some valid reasons to know who is holding and transacting in CBDCs.

Privacy is different from anonymity. Privacy is the right to keep personal or business data secret unless there is specific reason for its release. Anonymity is the absence of information revealing the party involved.

Some commentators hold that CBDCs increase central control over money and thus are a threat to freedom. This sentiment was certainly prevalent among many early adopters of bitcoin and remains fairly common today.

From the beginning, the promise of anonymity in holding and using cryptoassets appealed to many. Criminals of course loved the idea, but others saw a promise of complete personal privacy, a means to avoid governmental intrusion, or something that fit libertarian political leanings. The advocates of anonymity still exist and sometimes speak with great stridency.

Issuers of CBDCs will face pressures to create nearly-anonymous systems, to strictly limit legal powers to investigate cryptoassets, and allow holding of anonymous private instruments. Countries will need to prepare for political pressures and legal challenges. CBDC advocates are advised to be proactive in taking steps that assure the public that privacy will be protected.[98]

---

[98] Existing legal rules can have gaps or poorly describe digital practices. Legal battles can be expected following issuance of CBDCs, as shown in the European review of laws related to cryptoassets (see Chapter 4, above) and

Limitations on privacy and anonymity

CBDCs carry information on transactions and the parties involved, encoded to prevent unnecessary exposure of the information. However, there are commercial, policy, and legal reasons to access the information they carry. In some cases, aggregate information that does not reveal specific identifies is adequate, but at times there are reasons to drill down to individual transactions and identities.

CBDCs in commercial transactions

The general rules that apply to cryptoasset transactions and transfers can be expected to apply to CBDCs. CBDCs will need to be identifiable and carry along identification of their owner and payments characteristics in order to operate within the digital payments infrastructure.

Most importantly, this involves applying the FATF 'Travel Rule' that states that entities sending and receiving cryptoassets above a threshold must exchange information on the sender and recipient, perform checks verifying the identities of the parties making the exchange, and check that the parties are not under sanctions and thus ineligible to make the transaction. This rule guarantees that parties and exchanges involved in crypto transactions are known and traceable.

FATF Travel Rule

The Travel Rule is Recommendation 16 of the FATF (Financial Action Task Force) 40 recommendations to combat money laundering and financing of terrorism. It applies to any crypto transactions over a specified amount (which apparently is not yet set, but might be around $3000). The Rule can be expected to apply to CBDCs to ensure they are not misused. It applies to banks, other financial institutions, *and* other

---

uncertainty in the United States about whether instruments fall under securities or commodities trading regulations. Every country issuing CBDCs must review its legal and regulatory framework and institutions (and tax laws) and make changes as necessary. How is outside this book's scope, but it must be done.

entities exchanging cryptoassets (called VASPs – Virtual Asset Service Providers).

The Rule subjects cryptoasset transactions to multiple checks. An exchange sending a cryptoasset must (1) verify the sender's identity, (2) verify the recipient's identity, (3) check whether the recipient is under sanction, (4) perform due diligence on the receiving bank or exchange, then (5) transmit the identity of the sender to the recipient's exchange. In return, the recipient's exchange must take matching counterpart actions regarding the sender and sending exchange. After both sides complete all checks, the transaction can proceed.

These are extensive requirements that can take a while to ascertain, but for established banks acting for known customers, actions can be made digitally in an instant.

Over time, CBDCs are likely to be increasingly embedded into commercial wallets offered by banks and payment services. The CBDC could be a stand-alone part of the wallet, or might be programmed to meld with wallets' functions. For example, the e-CYN is designed to be programmed to fit carriers' needs so long as monetary policy aspects or other public functions are unchanged. (PBOC 2021) Wallets might begin replacing common existing electronic payments tools (credit and debit cards, phone banking, online payments) and the wallets themselves might be enhanced to facilitate commercial actions. For example, in the East Caribbean Currency Union the DCash CBDC was enhanced to facilitate record keeping and reconciliation of transactions between vendors and customers. Other commercial information can be included such as recording interest receipts, tax payments, initiating recurring payments, estimating fees and commissions, restoring lost funds, recording loyalty points, refunding returns, etc.

Two-tier CBDC schemes leave the interface with the public to bank and other payments firms. This option levers vendors' skills in marketing and innovating products to mass markets and customizing products for market niches. With their access to a great deal of customer information related to CBDCs, steps are needed to ensure that banks and exchanges do not violate customers' privacy (such as selling information to commercial marketers). Ideally, the vendors will use their information to create new services to help make the financial system more innovative, competitive, and robust. Some legal restrictions on banks' and vendors' data collected from CBDC transactions might be needed. In this commercial context, banks and payments firms continue to have their regular detailed commercial information and the central bank might only have aggregate information on CBDC transactions with private vendors.

Policy reasons to limit CBDC privacy

CBDC information can also be valuable for policy purposes because data are available very quickly with full detail if permitted. This helps monitor the impacts and effectiveness of policies, and can allow rapid responses.

Traditionally, macroeconomic policy was largely based on aggregate statistical data (money stock, interest rates, balance of payments, with disaggregation by major sector). Data from CBDCs can help compile such aggregates (that usually keep individual data confidential).

In contrast, the recent 'macroprudential' perspective often examines the robustness or vulnerabilities of individual banks. Detailed CBDC information can help evaluate the sector's condition, and if appropriate, can drill down to "systemically important banks" (SIBs) whose condition could affect the soundness of the entire sector. CBDC-based data could be part of enhanced macroprudential supervision even down to individual banks.[99]

CBDCs can also be subject to policy limitations and directives; limits on holdings or transactions per month, limits on foreign transactions, avoiding illegal or proscribed actions, or monitoring sanctions on countries or firms, etc.

---

[99] The central bank will already have information on its interactions with banking and financial institutions. Integrating CBDCs into the mix is not new in spirit, but it might provide greater speed and granularity into the process.

Banks are obligated under international rules to exercise due diligence that their financial activities are not used for criminal activity. Every bank is expected to apply "Know your customer" (KYC), "Anti-Money Laundering" (AML), and "Countering the Financing of Terrorism" (CFT) rules. Accounts should not be opened without verifying customers' identities, nor should funds be accepted from or lent for suspected criminal activity. CBDCs should have parallel rules, with a bonus possibility of better monitoring of misuse or infractions.

Authorities need access to CBDC information for criminal investigations and prosecutions. Many crimes can be attacked by "following the money", which CBDCs might facilitate. Ideally, countries place legal safeguards over spurious searches and misuse or unauthorized release of customer's information. CBDC regulations will probably need to specify when and how CBDC data can be used for such purposes.

Multiple country authorities seem to be converging on the view that smaller CBDC holdings and transactions probably should have privacy shields. The head of the Bank of England's CBDC section has said that the public will access a digital pound through private financial institutions who must have customer data and the BoE would not receive "personally identifiable information". (Dorrell 2023) The Chinese yuan CBDC (called the e-CNY) has different types of wallets permissioned based on the holder's identity that are programmed to carry out different functions. (PBOC 2021)

Digital Identities

Digital identities will be needed to access the varying features of CBDC wallets and access and control many other financial services. Wallets can exist with different limits on CBDC holdings or transactions restrictions for different classes of customers who must be unambiguously identified. Classes of customers could include financial institution, commercial company, government bodies, verified bank customers of a bank, users with limited on-line communications, foreign visitors, tax-free diplomats, etc.

The rules and classes of CBDC holders and wallets will vary between countries, but some sort of identity is needed for commercial purposes, tax and legal reasons, to receive government benefits, and possibly for policy reasons such as limiting transfers to foreign wallets or to sanctioned countries.

EU Revision of Digital ID Regulation

The EU has a very ambitious legislative proposal to upgrade its digital identity rules to create a union-wide system for financial transactions, legal attestations, medical records, and other services. A "once only" principle will apply in which the public and businesses need provide data to authorities only once. (European Parliament 2022)

Users will be able to verify their identities and transact, but can also verify the identities of counterpart companies and transactors. Privacy is built into the system so that users can control who has access to their data and the types of data available.

The program is very ambitious seeking digital access to all key public services with a goal that 80 percent of citizens will use it by 2030. The digital euro will be the means of payment in the system.

The mechanics of establishing a digital identity will be challenging, especially in economies with large informal markets, populations with limited on-line access, and less digitized financial systems. In such situations, unregistered CBDC wallets on handheld devices or mobile phones with limits on holdings or transactions might be emphasized.

Chapter 9. Monetary Policy and Financial Stability

The monetary policy and financial stability implications of CBDCs are big topics worthy of the efforts of great thinkers. These topics far transcend the pages of this small book.

The policy topics most covered in studies to date (June 2023) are reductions in cash use, shifts in central bank balance sheets and seigniorage income, disintermediation and destabilizing bank runs, and ease of cross-border shifts between currencies and exchange rate volatility.

This is a new area with great uncertainties. Experience is very limited because only a few countries have launched CBDCs and only within the past 3 years.

Lukonga in an IMF Working Paper (2023) gives perhaps the best available discussion of how CBDCs might affect monetary policy implementation and transmission. She concludes

"CBDCs do not change the objectives of monetary policy, nor change the operational framework for monetary policy, but they can engender changes in retail, wholesale, and cross-border payments that can have negative spillover effects on monetary policy implementation and transmission."

She cites possible implications for monetary policy;

- Induce changes in cash holdings and deposits that can disintermediate banks, affect monetary velocity, and increase volatility of bank reserves at the central bank.
- Weaken credit and interest rate channels of monetary policy transmission.
- Impair ability to conduct Open Market Operations (OMO) and thus weaken monetary adjustments and inflation targeting policy.
- Segment financial markets which can affect liquidity management and transmission of monetary policy impulses.
- Facilitate cross-border capital flows that could increase potential for currency substitution,

- Speed shifts in capital flows and their reversals that can impair control of the money stock and exchange rate policies.

- Analysis of these issues and more, backed up by extensive empirical data gathering and statistics, is needed. Investigations could be complex;

- Answers might depend on a country's financial structure, the specifics of the CBDC design, macroeconomic robustness, and legal and supervisory arrangements.

- Conclusions might depend on the specific CBDC design, a country's macroeconomic situation, balance of payments, financial sector soundness, competition from private cryptoassets, and quality of financial supervision, etc.

- Answers can be expected to differ for wCBDCs, rCBDCs, and platforms used for cross-border CBDC payments.

- Impacts on behavior and policy should be examined (1) as CBDCs are being issued and begin changing markets, (2) during the steady state when CBDCs are established, and (3) during crises.

- Reexaminations will be needed as new technologies emerge and legal and international standards and supervisory rules change.

Tokenized Markets and Monetary Policy

Tokenization represents an asset (deposit, security, commodity, etc.) in a digital form that allows their instant electronic trading just like other digital instruments. A bank, for example, could tokenize a tranche of its deposits to allow its trading in interbank markets.

Potentially, tokenization could grow rapidly affecting CBDCs directly or possibly enabling stablecoins or other private digital rivals. "The potential impacts of tokenized markets on monetary policy are not yet comprehensively understood." (Lukonga 2023)

Speed of CBDC Adoption – Monetary and stability effects will depend on the extent and speed of CBDC adoption. Limited adoption results in little domestic monetary or balance of payments consequences.

As described in Chapter 3, CBDC adoption thus far has been slow, so impacts have been minor. The slow uptake of rCBDCs is disappointing to some country officials seeking more rapid adoption to address some pressing needs. The factor for slow adoption most cited is overall satisfaction of much of the public with current payment practices, including mobile phone banking. Great hopes that rCBDCs will promote extensive financial inclusion have only been partially fulfilled. Many officials are certainly hoping for steadily more adoption.

Disintermediation – A key concern about rCBDCs is that the public will shift to holding them in lieu of putting deposits in the banking system. That cuts funding to the financial intermediaries that provide safe-keeping, depositing and lending services and are key for the implementation of monetary policy. Shrinkage of banks' balance sheets can reduce their lending and depress economic activity. In the extreme, the soundness of banks and even the stability of the entire financial system can be threatened.

The potential for disintermediation has been perhaps the most common area of research. Estimates of the degree of disintermediation have drawn varying conclusions, but at this point there is too little experience to draw firm conclusions.[100] One fairly common official conclusion about rCBDCs is that they should not be remunerated so that they are more cash like and don't compete with interest-paying deposit accounts.

Lukonga (2023) concludes that the disintermediation threat is greatest in banking systems with concentrations of small retail and demand deposits, low levels of digital payments, and in countries with weak

---

[100] As examples, Morgan Stanley estimated that a digital euro would supplant up to 8% of bank deposits (Jones 2021); a Bank of England study reviewed implications of a 20-percent shift from banks into CBDCs (Partington 2021); an IMF working paper by Gross and Letizia (2023) has a model to predict the degree of deposit disintermediation based on CBDC design features and extent of remuneration of the CBDC.

macroeconomic conditions.[101] These conditions are most likely in small- and medium-sized emerging economies where financial inclusion needs are great, but unfortunately also where resources are often limited.

Runs – Runs are large sudden withdrawals of assets placed in financial institutions often caused by lack of confidence in the institution and fears that deposits cannot be retrieved – thus threatening institutions' liquidity and stability. Runs on currency are also possible leading to sharp depreciation. The high tradability of digital instruments can increase the rapidity and intensity of runs and thus impair authorities' ability to smooth monetary conditions or stabilize exchange rates.[102]

Cocirculation and Currency Substitution – Small- and medium-size economies can be threatened by penetration of CBDCs from larger countries that circulate alongside domestic CBDCs and money, with many monetary and financial stability effects.[103] Cocirculation is a manner of currency substitution which is a shift from preferences for domestic currency assets to assets denominated in other currencies – CBDCs could facilitate rapid cross-border shifts between currencies. Cocirculation can impair central bank control over domestic monetary conditions

---

[101] She also concludes that Islamic banks are vulnerable due to concentrations of small deposits on their balance sheets.

[102] In the United States in 2023, Silicon Valley Bank and several other banks failed largely due to rapid remote transfers of deposits out of the banks The rapid onset of the run was little noticed at first, implying a need to upgrade official monitoring of banks to keep pace with digitalized banking.

A run on a bank or banking system (or private stablecoin) creates problems if banks lack the liquidity or sufficient reserves to cover withdrawals. Central banks have an option as lender-of-last-resort of extending emergency loans to troubled banks to help them survive. (In contrast for example, a run on a CBDC in exchange markets has different effects – the central bank can always issue more CBDCs, but this can have inflationary, exchange rate, or other impacts.)

[103] For more on cocirculation, see (Krueger and Ha 1995) and Krueger (2022).

and reduce seigniorage. Lukonga (p.20) concludes that currency substitution into CBDCs has the same economic effects as traditional cocirculation, but it can be facilitated by the fast pace and potentially larger scale of CBDCs.

Seigniorage – Cash use supports the seigniorage income of the central bank and government. Seigniorage is the earning on the assets received by the central bank or government from the public to purchase physical cash. Seigniorage income can be large, sometimes several percent of GDP. It is usually used to support central bank operations with any surplus transferred to the central government as the legal owner of the central bank.

Globally, cash use has been declining (thus cutting central bank income) as the public switches to electronic payments methods. Issuing an rCBDC could accelerate the ongoing secular declines in cash use, but public purchases of rCBDCs counters the cash drop, thus helping stabilize the central bank's finances.[104] Moreover, Khiaonarong and Humphrey (2022) on the 'marginal revealed preference for cash substitutes' argue that many of the new electronic payments platforms serve different functions from cash and do not actually compete with it – which suggests that by issuing CBDCs the central bank is moving into new areas of activity that could bolster the bank's financial condition.[105]

International Connections – CBDCs are seen as one of a range of tools that can significantly improve international financial transactions. They can be transmitted instantaneously across international borders and as riskless central bank money are readily accepted and settled.

---

[104] However, different transactions velocity of cash and CBDC can differ which can affect overall public money demand and affect seigniorage.

[105] They also find a preference for cash among older people while younger people prefer digital instruments – a demographic shift that likely will be accelerated by CBDCs.

However, CBDCs potentially can disrupt monetary policies of both the sending and receiving countries. Rapid international financial flows and their potential sharp reversal affect monetary policies in both countries. Some countries have responded with steps to preserve 'monetary sovereignty' – prevent foreign CBDCs from entering as well as preventing nonresidents from holding the domestic CBDC.

Major International Payments Enhancements

CBDC improvements to international payment infrastructure are not in isolation, but complement other impressive upgrades already in progress as described in Chapter 6. CBDCs are one part of multiple ongoing international efforts to increase throughput of international transactions, reduce costs, and guarantee rapid settlement.

As noted in Chapter 5, the G20 Roadmap for Enhancing Cross-Border Payments seeks to create fast, inexpensive, and inclusive cross-border financial services. CBDCs and global stablecoins are both recognized as potentially playing roles. Other international organizations have adopted the Roadmap and have actively moved to implement it. A Cross-Border Payments Coordination Group monitors implementation. (FSB 2022)

A key goal is to create international principles to harmonize and guide countries efforts. Individual countries can design their own Instant Payment Service then link it to a CBDC-based platform that transacts with a parallel system in another country. Thus, international payments platforms designed around digital tools are quickly emerging that will be relevant for countries' designs of their CBDC systems.

These initiatives highlight the payments aspects of CBDCs as potentially revolutionary to national and international financial policy.

Operational Risks – An important requirement of international bank supervisory standards is that banks hold additional capital to compensate for damage from 'operational risk'. Operational risk comprises threats to banks arising from problems with the effective and safe operation of the bank. These can include processing errors, breakdown of systems, internal fraud, cyber threats (hacking, denial of service attacks, poor governance, etc.), loss of power, loss of phone or computer connections, poor security, etc. CBDCs can suffer from similar problems.[106]

Operational risk increases as CBDC adoption increases. If an rCBDC replaces most cash or checking deposits, an operational collapse like a three-day communications loss will be a massive economic catastrophe.

Dealing with operational risk requires creating redundancy and back-up facilities. Files must be stored off-site and can be restored and possibly funds returned. These are expensive requirements that might strain resources of some countries.

Growing Pains and Failing Expectations – Authorities will need to weather problems that will affect new complex systems, slow adoptions, cost overruns, human error, and possible public disappointment that promises of important digital advances are slow arriving. Confidence in authorities' and central bank' policies might deteriorate with political repercussions. Also, the speed with which CBDCs can be transacted might affect markets faster than authorities can monitor and take corrective action.

If problems arise, did they come from the CBDC system and are correctable, were poor operations by the system vendor responsible, or did they arise from normal macroeconomic economic and financial fluctuations for which the new CBDCs are innocent – but easily blamable – bystanders? Faced with problems, authorities need to accurately identify causes and solutions. Close oversight during the implementation period by technical experts, international and regional bodies, with required public reports of experiences will be valuable. The experiences of other countries can be compared. And more academic analyses of monetary and financial soundness implications can be expected.

---

[106] Operational problems have also plagued many private cryptoassets.

Unknowns – Many policy and stability implications of CBDCs are still unknown, both in general and as specifically applied to individual country situations, system designs, and legal and supervisory frameworks.

Some topics that have received attention have been noted above. Less is known about impacts on central bank balance sheets and seigniorage, money stock, velocity, sensitivity to interest rates, exchange rate volatility, cross-border CBDC flows, use by financial actors outside existing monetary policy control mechanisms, and resilience of CBDCs against competition from quasi-monetary private cryptoassets. Serious work is undoubtedly underway on these and other issues, but until there is more experience in the field many unknowns will continue.

It is yet not possible to know whether the CBDC impacts will be in line with existing policy or whether they raise new policy challenges. It might take several years' work to resolve some of the current unknowns.

Blurring between Monetary and Other Financial Instruments

Chapter 5 describes how digitalization and tokenization of financial assets is blurring the lines between CBDCs as monetary financial instruments, digital assets, and traditional deposits, loans, and securities. In particular, stablecoins that promise fixed rates against national currency, rapid and inexpensive transactions, final settlement, etc. might actively compete with traditional money, change public monetary behavior, and affect policy.

Policy implications of this blurring are unknown. Are measures of money stock and growth affected? Is velocity changed? How quickly are monetary policy actions transmitted into private financial markets? How is cross-border transmission of monetary policy affected?

A lot needs to be learned – many regressions rerun – perhaps old policy paradigms will be tossed or new ones born.

To summarize, the monetary and financial stability issues surrounding CBDCs are only beginning to be researched in depth. Moreover, CBDCs are recent and exist in only a few countries so there is little empirical experience to draw on.

Sharing CBDC Experiences

Far too little is known about the actual experiences and possible impacts of CBDCs. Lots of countries are simultaneously piloting or issuing CBDCs. As experience is gained (positive, negative, expected or unexpected), every country that issues or is working on CBDCs should provide in-depth reviews *with statistics* at least once a year. The analyses and discussions will inform the public and the CBDC community at large, and guide oversight and legislative bodies. The public, businesses, and financial markets will better understand how to prepare. Fellow countries will benefit, best practices can be shared, and international rules makers will have a better basis for their deliberations.

More needs to be said than can be conveyed in a few paragraphs in the central bank annual report. Central banks and payments officials can say far more to each other than can be conveyed to the public – topical or regional committees and hubs are a good option.

On one hand, enhanced speed, lower costs, security, and firm settlement are transformative benefits of CBDCs that benefit consumers and promote inclusion, could bring substantial macroeconomic benefits, and accelerate economic development.

On the other hand, risks to policy and soundness must be taken seriously. At present, major countries such as the United States, United Kingdom, Euroarea, and Japan are taking cautious approaches to allow time to analyze technical and policy issues and design systems that are beneficial, safe, and resilient.

Conversely, many countries want rapid adoption of rCBDCs to serve their populations' needs for better financial services. Reconciling these desires with legitimate uncertainties about policy and financial stability and the deliberate pace of key major countries and the IMF CBDC handbook is difficult. Moreover, very rapid improvements in domestic and cross-border payments systems are underway and CBDC systems should keep pace with the best international payments standards to be able to link to those systems. It might be prudent to move cautiously although that could become politically painful. At a suitable time, country implementation will be supported by ample international advice and assistance to smooth and accelerate the major transformations ahead.

Rethinking Optimum Currency Area (OCA) Theory?

The Noble Prize-winning concept of Optimum Currency Areas was developed by Robert Mundell in 1961. OCA states that separate countries can successfully operate using a single currency only if they exhibit a high degree of macroeconomic convergence. OCA theory underpins the rules for membership in the European Monetary System and other regional monetary initiatives.[107]

However, Harold, Landau, and Brunnermeier (2019) argue that digitalization can foster new forms of currency areas from the traditional OCA concept. Competition between currencies "will no longer be based mainly on macroeconomic (inflation) performance." Convergence and harmonization of financial policy might fade into insignificance given the ability to transact digitally and use a network measure of value (such as stablecoins or within private networks).

They state that private digital networks can link financial activities without regard to national borders. "Digitalization may thus serve as a powerful vehicle to internationalize some currencies as media of exchange."

Digitalization can often include fostering penetration of financial systems by other countries' currencies. Among their conclusions are "The best defense against digital dollarization may be for countries to issue their own currencies in digital form by creating central bank digital currencies (CBDCs)."

---

[107] See Krueger (2022, Chapter 3) on OCA and some reconsiderations of it.

Chapter 10. Small Country and Regional Issues

Smaller economies face challenges regarding CBDCs, whether wCBDCs or rCBDCs. Their financial systems can be small and uncompetitive compared to their larger neighbors, access to many financial services might be limited, and services might be costly. CBDCs might solve some of the problems, but the country might be short of the expertise and resources to design, build, and operate a robust and secure system. Also, their CBDCs will compete with CBDCs of larger neighbors – cocirculation of other countries' CBDCs within small economies is a possibility.

As mentioned in Chapter 3, many smaller countries have approached the IMF about how to create CBDCs. In April 2023, the IMF (2023) reported on how it will provide 'capacity development' (CD) assistance to such countries.[108]

A problem with CBDCs is that it is technologically easy and quick to create them, but far more difficult to build a system that effectively serves the public, is reliable, is operationally secure, does not create financial instability, fits monetary and balance of payments policy needs, and has effective supervision and legal protection.

Countries need to build their own capacity (or find ways to work cooperatively with others) to evaluate options and design systems that meet their specific situations and policy goals. Operations might be left partially to outside vendors, but good oversight will be needed. This is not easy and can be time consuming. The IMF is preparing a Handbook on CBDCs to help countries and other international and regional bodies. It

---

[108] In 2021, the IMF set up a strategic plan for digital assets to help ensure the stability of the international monetary system, promote member countries' financial stability, and facilitate international monetary cooperation. The review covered CBDCs and other digital money (such as private stablecoins) in matters such as international capital flows, global payments systems, international reserves, monetary policy, and crisis intervention. (2021)

can also give guidance and sometimes financial support. The IMF says it will take 3-to-5 years to understand early experiences with CBDCs, evaluate options, and *write* the handbook – which indicates that the CBDC process done properly is complex and impactful and thus should be approached with prudence.

Scenarios

Below several scenarios are presented about how smaller countries might go about creating CBDCs. A tension revealed in the scenarios is the urge to quickly address pressing needs can clash with the tasks involved to build effective, secure, robust systems.

A first step is setting priorities before designing CBDC systems. Among priorities that smaller central banks have cited are:

- enhance financial inclusion
- facilitate remittances and lower their cost
- integrate financial markets
- adopt digital financial technology to increase market efficiency
- facilitate cross-border transactions and settlement
- use as a monetary policy tool
- counter decreased use of cash
- maintain seigniorage income
- bolster financial stability
- defend monetary sovereignty against penetration by other CBDCs, stablecoins, and cryptoassets.

Given multiple priorities, which CBDC scenarios are most likely and how might their prospects be affected by their choice? The following scenarios indicate markedly different paths that countries might choose given their priorities and technical resources.

A very important consideration for all countries – and especially smaller and emerging economies – is whether they have the technical expertise and resources to evaluate CBDC options, effectively operate the system, adapt monetary and balance of payments policies, and deal with risks and problems that arise. System failures in more vulnerable economies could be especially severe. Many countries will need assistance to design and operate their CBDC system – in addition to contracted resources and expertise, assistance might come from regional development banks, currency unions[109], payment systems such as SWIFT, or the international financial organizations.

Scenario 1: No Coordination

In broad terms, Emerging Market and Developing Economies (EMDEs) prioritize financial inclusion and cutting remittances costs while politically capturing some of the enthusiasm surrounding cryptoassets. These priorities could induce some countries to independently go forward with domestic rCBDC schemes. Pioneer CBDCs have shown that technically some form of system can be introduced quickly, which makes introducing a CBDC a tempting political option. There also seems to be some tendency to promote domestic businesses to launch the CBDC.

Within any particular region, multiple countries could independently develop retail CBDCs – for example, the e-Naira and e-Cedi in Nigeria and nearby Ghana. These efforts might divert focus away from deepening regional financial integration or unions. Multiple nonharmonized CBDCs could have diverse impacts on their home countries and complicate cross-border transactions within the region.[110]

---

[109] Just over half of all countries are now in, or are working to create, a currency union. Currency unions potentially can play a key role in supporting CBDC development. Unions work to develop a common monetary policy and integrate regional financial systems, which would be supported by a common CBDC. Also, labor migration within regions generates cross-country remittances that would benefit from access to a common CBDC.

[110] Both countries are part of the West African Monetary Zone (WAMZ) which plans to create a common currency and thus would have a single union-wide CBDC.

In this scenario, CBDCs can provide domestic benefits, but the independent experiments undertaken so far suggest that countries must take significant actions to guard against various risks:

- Monetary and exchange rate policies and financial conditions can be affected by the speed, ease of shifting assets, and anonymity provided by CBDCs.
- An effective outreach campaign is needed to build public and business acceptance.
- Businesses must learn now to process CBDCs, detect counterfeits, and change their accounting and finance systems.
- Fraud, counterfeiting, and criminal abuses are possible, especially when the CBDC is being introduced and for technologically unsophisticated populations.
- The technical ease of creating a CBDC might outrun the design and building of fundamental arrangements critical to the success of a CBDC, Strong market infrastructures, supervisory and legal frameworks, and monetary and balance of payments policies are needed.
- Even relatively small-scale independent CBDCs must take cyber and operational risks seriously, which means creating redundancy and backup arrangements and permitting restitution of public and business losses from operational failures. These can be expensive precautions.
- The ability of individual small country CBDCs to successfully compete against major outside CBDCs or stablecoins is unknown. If digital euros, dollars, yuan, or stablecoins become deeply embedded outside their home countries, monetary control could be impaired. [111]

---

[111] An IMF review of CBDC projects in Latin America says that "CBDCs issued by advanced countries could negatively affect emerging markets by increasing pressures for currency substitution and reducing the scope for monetary policy, including the ability to enforce exchange restrictions and capital flow management measures." (2023, p. 8)

Countries must carefully weigh benefits, costs, and risks from retail CBDCs, and whether the country infrastructure can support the many aspects of CBDCs. Introducing a CBDC could prove economically and politically intolerable if it is not publicly accepted, creates financial risks and instabilities, impairs monetary control, or fails operationally. Creating an independent CBDC might not be feasible for some countries. It might also complicate existing or future regional monetary arrangements.

Fortunately, a lot of information is available from early experiments and ongoing research in the Euroarea and elsewhere. Active work by the IMF, BIS, SWIFT, and other international organizations has begun to set standards and outline feasible approaches.

Scenario 2: Link to CBDC Cross-Border Projects

If m-CBDC Bridge, Project Aurum, Project Icebreaker, Project Nexus, or similar arrangements (See Chapter 6) become feasible, many CBDC cross-border complications might fade away. These schemes channel cross-border transactions into a common system that exchanges national CBDCs to provide riskless, instantaneous, transactions with full finality. Commercial banks and other businesses can link to the system which can permit nearly seamless customer to business retail or person-to-person transactions across borders.

The systems allow national CBDCs to be treated as separate monetary arrangements with flexibility to exchange between countries. Countries can maintain 'monetary sovereignty' with own monetary policies and capturing seigniorage.

Once the schemes are set up, it is advantageous for countries to create CBDCs for use in cross-border transactions, rather than use the prevailing international correspondent bank system that is slower and more expensive.

Such systems will standardize CBDC messaging procedures between sending and receiving countries. Countries, their banks, and entities transmitting CBDCs will need to adopt the common standards. This might be done with only a small group of countries (discussions between Argentina and Brazil might produce a two-country system), but a scheme could become a single international standard. By incorporating international minimum requirements, individual country CBDCs might become easily tradable with those of other countries. How such arrangements might develop is beyond this book.

By linking to a cross-border CBDC system, domestic markets benefit from the national CBDC, but country cross-border frictions can be eased, fewer intermediary payment service providers are needed, settlement is instantaneous and final, cross-border transactions' costs reduced. Also, the system makes permanent records of transfers, which can be useful for reporting to clients, policy analysis, and statistical purposes. [112]

Schemes are complex because some harmonization of domestic and cross-border payments and settlements systems between financial institutions is required.

The Saudi/UAE Project Aber was an early successful test along these lines (SAMA 2020).[113] More recently, the m-CBDC Bridge project now

---

[112] An unknown regarding these schemes is whether they will tend to reduce cocirculation of foreign CBDCs or foreign currencies in an economy. In principle, the schemes could make it more convenient to transact only in the domestic currency even for cross-border transactions, but other motivations could prove important such as concern about inflation differentials, interest rates, distrust of the national currency, banking sector weakness, etc.

[113] Project Aber involved two countries whose currencies were already linked in the Gulf Cooperation Council (GCC) quasi-monetary union. It used a joint CBDC created by the Saudi and UAE central banks. Aber tested payments

(continued)

under way between four unlinked currencies (China, Hong Kong, Thailand, and the UAE) shows the model might have global applicability.

Global CBDC-Ledger System?

The possibility of a common CBDC-based international payments arrangement has been raised by Carstens (2023), which he describes as a "unified programmable ledger in a public-private partnership." Central banks would create CBDCs to populate efficient payment systems and cross-border linkages; banks and other market institutions would interface with the public to offer innovative digital services and create "tokenized deposits"; and a unified digital ledger would record and settle transactions and holdings.[114] [115]

This describes a potentially global system that leverages CBDC digital efficiency and low costs, operated under guidance of the central banking community in accordance with international best practices, to provide inclusive and secure financial coverage. "Any sequence of transactions in programmable money can be automated and seamlessly integrated.

Such a scheme would be a major transformative initiative of the international financial community – something that appears increasingly plausible.

---

between financial institutions within a country and in different countries with ensured settlement on each end of the transaction.

[114] The Carstens proposal appears decendent from Project Helvetia, which was an early exploration by the Swiss National Bank and the BIS Innovation Hub in Switzerland to test integration of tokenized assets and central bank money. One path tested use of a CBDC on a permissioned DLT platforms, and another tested settlement using a digital exchange and the existing central bank payment system – both methods were found successful. Also, linking DLT systems with settlement in riskless CBDCs was viewed as facilitating operation of Centralized Securities Databases (CSDs).

[115] See also IMF (2022d).

Scenario 3: Single Union-wide CBDC System

A monetary union comprises a very wide range of tasks and policies - currency, monetary policy, interest rates, exchange rates, payments, integration of financial markets, and supervision, among others. A single CBDC will prevail in a union. It must be designed to fit seamlessly into all aspects of the union.

In Scenario 2, above, it is suggested that countries might have less interest in creating a currency union because innovative payments features of CBDCs can achieve many purposes of a monetary union. However, scenario 3 suggests that CBDCs could actually accelerate union building.

> Perhaps the most important reason is that many smaller countries have insufficient resources or technical expertise to design, operate, and supervise a CBDC system. Their hope of having a CBDC might rest in cooperating with other nearby countries.[116]

Some regions have a large dominant economy and surrounding countries are unlikely to independently successfully compete against a regional giant. Monetary linking of smaller countries in a region with the dominant economy might de facto be the only feasible option.

Payments Unions or Currency Unions?

If the various cross-border CBDC systems live up to their early promise, they could become widespread. With endpoints in different countries encompassed in the system, these schemes achieve many of the features of cross-border frictionless financial transfer aspects sought in currency unions.

---

[116] During preparations for the European Monetary Union, topical committees involving all potential countries met regularly, surveyed national resources and problems, made decisions on how to move forward, monitored results, and – very importantly – kept pressure on laggard countries to keep making progress. Similar regional arrangements for CBDCs would be valuable.

Currency unions strive to make cross-border transactions as smooth and quick as possible in order to unify monetary and financial markets and facilitate transmission of monetary policy impulses across the union. In true unions, like the ECCU or EMU, a single monetary policy using a common CBDC will be used. But if a CBDC-based 'payments union' built on a CBDC arrangement can quickly provide many of the advantages of monetary union, it could become preferred to taking the highly complex path to full monetary union.[117]

Among other reasons for promoting financial integration in a currency union could include;

- Counter pressures from outside CBDCs or private cryptoassets
- Capture efficiencies of a union-wide digital monetary instrument
- Stabilize markets from common policies and mutual support
- Avoid expense of operating a CBDC system alone
- Create an economically larger space providing more opportunities for national business
- Facilitate regional labor movement and remittances
- Deal with cross-border CBDC counterfeiting or fraud.
- Benefit from joint decision-making and problem-solving
- Accede to the economic power of larger regional countries and seek to enter that market.

Explorations under way in the East African Community (EAC) to improve the operations of its regional cross-border payments system highlight how CBDCs might promote currency union prospects (Bitcoinke.io 2021) (Saddam 2019). A common CBDC could integrate real-time gross settlement systems in all of the EAC's six member countries. It would

---

[117] Krueger (2022) describes the long road to create the European Monetary Union and what other regions can learn from it. *In short, if payments initiatives accomplish many goals of a monetary union quickly, help maintain monetary sovereignty, and limit difficult political implications, motivation to complete full-scale monetary unions could weaken.*

help overcome the limited stocks of partner member states' currencies available for settlement, fend off challenges from diverse national payment systems, and cure the lack of centralized liquidity and collateral management.[118]

To summarize, smaller countries will face many CBDC challenges. Countries might be gradually moving beyond the Scenario 1 phase to increasingly draw on international and regional advice and resources (as described in Scenario 2). A lot of work in the next three to five years might be as described under Scenario 2. Scenario 3 that takes a harmonized multi-country approach advances many aspects of Scenario 2 and provides broader benefits, but the process is more drawn out and might be politically more challenging.

---

[118] These issues are already being addressed in the Euroarea, but they are continuing challenges already recognized in developing the East African Community monetary union.

Chapter 11. Conclusions

Central Bank Digital Currencies (CBDCs) are the theme of this book, but they must be viewed in the context of the surge in digital financial instruments. Since the birth of bitcoin a decade and half ago, thousands of encrypted digital financial instruments have appeared. They serve a wide variety of functions with major impacts on economic behavior. The innovations continue and will thrive and evolve into the future.

CBDCs are a central banking response to the digital revolution. The idea of an electronic form of money has existed for decades, but the surge of private digital instruments with quasi-monetary characteristics threatened the space reserved for official money. Also, market volatility, misuse, and financial market disruptions from the new private instruments prompted changes in policy and supervision and ultimately central banks felt forced to move forward with official digital money. CBDCs were born.

CBDCs are still in their infancy. It is clear that they will eventually extend to nearly all countries and have pervasive effects on money and finance. Today only a few clues are available about what that world might look like. On one hand, caution in issuing CBDCs is prudent given the many unknowns and possible costly missteps. On the other hand, there are urges to act quickly to participate in the digital revolution, to counter threats to monetary policy from private digital instruments, and serve the public.

Amidst these uncertainties, this book draws some general conclusions.

CBDCs are complex and present many technical, policy, and practical challenges, especially for rCBDCs intended for use by the general public and business. It is emphasized that a CBDC is both a monetary instrument *and* a payments instrument that facilitates rapid, secure, and low-cost transactions. Thus, CBDCs will change how people perceive and use money, but equally important will open new channels for rapid, inexpensive, and secure transactions. Market practice, institutions, policies, and laws will change to accommodate both aspects of CBDCs.

The book looks at the evolution of digital assets and how CBDCs fit into the big picture. CBDCs will need to be innovative and serve the public in order to effectively compete with private digital assets and modern telecommunications and online payments methods.

A review of some early CBDC programs shows that to date public adoption has been rather slow. This might change but it suggests that much of the public is already pretty happy with their current payment services. A corollary is that many CBDC systems are being designed as two-tier systems to work through existing banking and payments channels – an approach that leverages the expertise of private partners to reach the public and keeps central banks out of areas where they have less experience.

Competitive Cost-Benefit Analysis

Launching CBDCs, especially rCBDCs, is costly. Systems must be designed, fit into existing payments methods, adjust or create monetary and international financial policies, reflect emerging international standards, change accounting and statistical systems, and make legal and institutional changes. Direct costs include purchasing new equipment, hiring technical staff, educating banks, businesses, and the public, and changing accounting standards. Policies and mechanisms need to be in place to deal with unexpected problems or crises, including contingent emergency lines-of-credit facilities.

Possibly offsetting these costs and tasks are gains in seigniorage, reduced cash processing costs, less cocirculation of foreign currencies within the economy, reduced administrative costs because of digitalization, better tax collection, or creation of new savings platforms. Potentially, there could be wide-spread gains in economic productivity, greater financial inclusion, high financial through-put, and less expensive cross-border remittances and payments.

The cost-benefit analysis can be highly dependent on the structure and demographics of each economy, the legal and supervisory framework, and state of the financial system. Competition from existing financial institutions and private cryptoassets could matter. Possibly, in some countries potential CBDC benefits can be gained by tweaking private digital instruments without needing to create CBDCs – explorations are already underway into CBDC-backed stablecoins that blur distinctions between central bank and commercial bank money.

As of mid-2023, the deliberate pace of CBDC investigations in many countries could reflect uncertainties about benefits and possible non-CBDC alternatives before plunging in to commit to the significant costs of launching CBDCs.[119]

As cited in Chapter 4, the European program for a future digital euro has shown the breadth of the supervisory, institutional, and legal issues surrounding CBDCs. Also covered are several international programs setting standards for covering cryptoassets' supervisory treatment and financial messaging. These examples show a partial model and standards that countries must act on in designing their CBDCs.

Several projects facilitating cross-border CBDC transactions are covered. This promising work allows countries to retain domestic controls over their CBDCS, but permits instantaneous, low-cost, exchanges of CBDC-based transactions across borders.

Monetary Sovereignty vs. Financial Integration

Cross-border CBDC systems designed to retain 'monetary sovereignty' while promoting efficient international transactions can however leave in place many frictions that affect cross-border commerce. These can stem from diverse policies and institutions between trading countries (different monetary policies, interest rates, trade documentation, supervisory rules, legal systems, dispute resolution procedures, phytosanitary rules, etc.).

Many of these frictions are already being addressed by a broad range of international rules, codes, and best practices, which are definitely helping harmonize and improve international commerce and financial

---

[119] By mid-2025, perhaps sooner, the cost-benefit calculations including the key variables might be much clearer.

conditions. Countries and regional bodies often voluntarily accede to the various international or regional practices.

At one end of the spectrum, in regional monetary unions (such as ECCU and EMU, and a cluster of nascent unions) monetary sovereignty is formally granted to the union. The union will seek to erase cross-border financial and other frictions in order to operate a single monetary, interest rate, and exchange rate policy across the union. And – remembering this book's theme – there will be only a single CBDC for all member countries.

The resultant picture is mixed. Nearly all countries are busy adopting various international rules; more than a hundred are working on CBDCs; and about half the globe's countries are in or are working towards monetary union. Simultaneously, cryptoassets are challenging all countries, regions, and international organizations. The CBDC story is mixed into all these situations. Monetary and payments conditions are profoundly changing in all countries creating interesting choices ahead about monetary sovereignty and international financial cooperation.

Chapter 7 focuses on issues related to retail CBDCs, how they can serve the public, and especially provide financial services to populations with limited access to formal banking. rCBDCs can be highly complex and politically sensitive because they serve so many diverse public needs – two long lists of issues are provided that countries should address in designing their rCBDC systems.

Privacy issues remain a key concern about CBDCs. Deep-rooted concerns that CBDCs might threaten individual and commercial privacy must be dealt with to successfully launch CBDCs. Many countries are planning to keep central banks remote from personal information on customers held by banks and financial institutions.

There are many concerns about the monetary policy and financial stability issues related to CBDCs. CBDCs are new, experience is very limited, empirical information is lacking, and academic theoretical work to date is limited. Chief concerns seem to be that CBDCs could draw funds away from banks, withdrawals could turn into runs due to the speed of digital transactions. Less is known about changes in central bank balance sheets and seigniorage, money stock, velocity, sensitivity to interest rates, exchange rate volatility, cross-border CBDC flows, use by financial actors outside existing monetary policy control mechanisms, and resilience of CBDCs against competition from quasi-monetary private cryptoassets. Blurring of distinctions between CBDCs and competitive stablecoins will be a continuing complication. Serious work is undoubtedly underway on these and other issues, but until there is more experience in the field many unknowns will continue.

Chapter 10 provides some scenarios for smaller countries designing their CBDC systems. As international standards and guidance develop further, countries are likely to increasingly draw on them and thus are less likely to independently build CBDC systems. Alternatively, countries might focus on developing rudimentary CBDCs that can be used in several new projects for efficient cross-border transactions. Also, regional cohesion might increase as smaller or less-developed countries draw guidance and resources from more powerful neighbors creating prospects for regional CBDC payments arrangements.

CBDCs and financial digitalization are creating massive changes to global financial systems. These are exciting times that offer great promise amidst numerous uncertainties and risks. Let us hope we do things right.

References

Adrian, T. (2019) "Stablecoins, Central Bank Digital Currencies, and Cross-Border Payments: A New Look at the International Monetary System" Remarks by Tobias Adrian at a IMF-Swiss National Bank Conference, Zurich. May 14, 2019.

_____ (2023) "Exploring Cross-Border and Domestic Payment and Contracting Platforms" Speech at Joint IMF-Bank Al-Maghrib High-Level Roundtable on Central Bank Digital Currencies. Rabat, Morocco, June 19 2023.

Adrian, T. and T. Mancini-Griffoli (2023) "The Rise of Payment and Contracting Platforms" IMF Fintech Note/2023/5 June 2023.

Atlantic Council. (2023) Online CBDC development tracker. www.atlantic-council.org/cbdctracker/.

Auer, R. and R. Böhme (2020) "The technology of retail central bank digital currency" BIS Quarterly Review, March 2020.

BIS (Bank for International Settlements) (2023) Lessons learnt on CBDCs. Report submitted to the G20 Finance Ministers and Central Bank Governors July 2023.

Bank of Botswana (2021). Statement on crypto assets – participation and regulation. Press Release. November 10, 2021.

Bank of England and HM Treasury. (2023) The digital pound: a new form of money for households and businesses? Consultation Paper. February 2023.

Barber, G. (2019). "The Fed Chair Says Facebook's Libra Raises 'Serious Concerns' " wired.com. July 10, 2019.

BCBS (Basel Committee for Banking Supervision). (2021) "Consultative Document: Prudential Treatment of Cryptoasset Exposures" June 2021.

_____ (2022) "Prudential Treatment of Cryptoasset Exposures". December 2022.

Berwick, A. and Wilson, T. (2023) "Crypto giant Binance commingled customer funds and company revenue, former insiders say" Reuters. May 23, 2023.

Bitcoinke.io (2021a) "The East African Community States to Explore Potential for a CBDC in a Move to Upgrade the Shared East African Payments System." Bitcoinke.io. June 2021.

_____ (2023) "We are working on a Global Platform" Speech by IMF Managing Director Kristalina Georgieva, Rabat Morocco, June 20 2023.

Bloomberg News. (2021) "China's Digital Yuan Expands to 10 Million Eligible Users" July 8, 2021.

_____ (2022a) "Ditch Bitcoin: IMF urges El Salvador to rethink crypto" January 25, 2022.

_____ (2022b) "El Salvador's companies barely bother with bitcoin" March 18, 2022.

Boar, C., and A. Wehrli. (2021) "Ready, steady, go? Results of the third BIS Survey on central bank digital currency." BIS Papers No. 114. January 2021.

Böhme et al (2015) (Böhme, R, Christin, N, Edelman, B, and Moore, T) "Bitcoin: Economics, Technology, and Governance" Journal of Economic Perspectives, Spring 2015.

Carstens, A. (2023) "Innovation and the future of the monetary system" Speech at Monetary Authority of Singapore. February 22, 2023.

Central Bank of Nigeria (2023) Payments System Vision 2025 CBN Website 2023.

CNBC.com (2021) "162 million up for grabs after bug in DeFi Protocol Compound" Oct. 3, 2021.

_____ (2022a) "A $3.5 billion bet on bitcoin becoming a 'reserve currency' for crypto is being put to the test" May 9, 2022.

_____ (2022b) "EU agrees to landmark legislation to clean up crypto 'Wild West' " June 30, 2022.

Coindesk.com. (2023) "China includes Digital Yuan in Cash Circulation Data for the First Time." January 11, 2023.

Cointelegraph.com (2023a). Nigeria to create legal framework for stablecoins and ICOs. January 10, 2023.

Cointelegraph.com (2023b) Nigeria revisits its payments landscape amid sluggish eNaira adoption" January 12, 2023.

Decentralized.trading (2021) "Bitcoin adoption could damage El Salvador's credit rating: Fitch" August 17, 2021.

Digitalpoundfoundation.com (2023) "MiCA's stablecoin transaction cap stifles crypto adoption, say lawyers" July 10, 2023.

Dorn, J. (2021) "China's Digital Yuan: A Threat to Freedom" Cato.org. August 25, 2021.

Dorrell, C. (2023) "BoE's CBDC head says digital pound will have the 'very highest standards of privacy' " digitalpoundfoundation.com. May 11, 2023.

ECB (European Central Bank) (1998) "Report on electronic money" August 1998.

_____ (2020) Report on digital Euro. October 2020.

_____ (2021a) "The ECB's monetary policy strategy statement" July 2021.

_____ (2021b) Digital euro project. July 2021.

ECB Crypto-Assets Task Force (2020) Stablecoins: Implications for monetary policy, financial stability, market infrastructure and payments, and banking supervision in the euro area. ECB Occasional Paper No. 247. September 2020.

ECCB (Eastern Caribben Central Bank) (2022) "Dcash Service Resumes" Press Release March 9, 2022.

European Union (2000) Directive 2000/46/EC of the European Parliament and of the Council "On the Taking up, Pursuit of and Prudential Supervision of the Business of Electronic Money Institutions".

EC (2020a) European Commission. "Proposal for a regulation ... on Markets in Crypto-assets" September 2020.

_____ (2020b) "Proposal for a regulation on a pilot regime for market infrastructures based on distributed ledger technology" September 2020.

Eckberg, J and Ho, M. "A New Dawn for Digital Currency" Oliver Wyman. 2021.

ESRB (2020) (European Systemic Risk Board) Systemic cyber risk. February 2020.

European Monetary Institute (EMI) (1998) "Opinion of the EMI Council on the Issuance of electronic money" transmitted to the Economic Commission, March 2, 1998. In EMI Annual Report 1997, pp 74-75.

European Parliament. (2022) "Revision of the eIDAS Regulation – European Digital Identity (EUid)" (2022).

Feng, C. (2023). "Jiangsu city leverages logistics hub status to promote c-CNY in Belt and Road Trade" scmp.com. April 23, 2023.

FRB. (2022). "Money and Payments: The U.S. dollar in the Age of Digital Transformation." January 20.

FSB (Financial Soundness Board) 2022. G20 Roadmap for Enhancing Cross-border Payments: Second Consolidated Progress Report. October 2022.

_____ (2023) FSB Global Regulatory Framework for Crypto-Asset Activities. July 17, 2023.

Gonzalez, M. (2021) "The surprising history of distributed ledger technology" medium.com. August 25, 2021.

Gross, M. and E. Letizia. (2023) "To Demand or Not to Demand: On Quantifying the Future Appetite for CBDC" IMF WP/23/9. January 2023.

Group of Central Banks. (2020) "Central bank digital currencies: foundational principles and core features" Joint Report, no 1, October 2020.

Harold, J., Landau, J-P, and Brunnermeier, M. (2019) "Digital Currency Areas" CEPR.org. July 3, 2019.

Hong Kong. (2021) Government of the Hong Kong Special Administrative Region. "Joint statement on Multiple Central Bank Digital Currency (m-CBDC) Bridge Project" Press Release. February 23, 2021.

IMF (2020) "Eastern Caribbean Currency Union: Selected Issues – A Central Bank Digital Currency for the ECCU" Country Report 20/71. March 2020.

_____ (2022a) "Eastern Caribbean Currency Union 2022 Article IV Consultation". Country Report No. 22/253. 2022.

_____ (2022b) "IMF Staff Completes Virtual Staff Visit to the Republic of Marshall Islands". IMF Press Release 22/18 April 13, 2022.

_____ (2022c) "IMF Releases the 2022 Financial Access Survey Results" Press Release. October 5, 2022.

124

_____ (2022d) "A Multi-currency Exchange and Contracting Platform" WP/22/217. November 2022.

_____ (2023) Crypto Assets and CBDCs in Latin America and the Caribbean: Opportunities and Risks. WP/23/37. February 2023.

IMF (International Monetary Fund) (2020) Digital Money Across Borders – Macro-Financial Implications. Policy Paper 2020/050. October 19, 2020.

_____ (2021) The Rise of Digital Money: A Strategic Plan to Continue Delivering On The IMF's Mandate. Policy Paper No. 2021/054. 2021.

_____ (2023) IMF Approach to Central Bank Digital Currency Capacity Development. IMF Staff Report Policy Paper 2023/016. April 10, 2023.

IOSCO (International Organization of Securities Commissions) (2023) Policy Recommendations for Crypto and Digital Asset Markets. CR01/2023. May 2023.

Jones, M. (2021) "Digital euro might suck away 8% of banks' deposits" Reuters. June 15 2021.

Kenya Central Bank (2023) "Issuance of Discussion Paper on Central Bank Digital Currency: Comments from the Public" Press Release. June 2, 2023.

Khiaonarong, T. and Humphrey, D. "Falling Use of Cash and Demand for Retail Central Bank Digital Currency" IMF Working Paper WP/22/27. February 2022.

Khmer Times. (2023) "Cambodia's Bakong Payment System used in Laotian CBDC proof-of-concept project" February 9, 2023.

Krueger, R. (2022) Building New Currency Unions: Lessons from the European Monetary Union. (ISBN 9 780578 266862).

Krueger, R., and Ha, J. (1995) "Measurement of the Cocirculation of Currencies." IMF Working Paper 95/34.

Kurian, A. (2023) "The Case for Harmonizing Central Bank Digital Currencies for Cross-Border Transactions" ORFOnline.org June 2023.

Ledgerinsights (2023a) "Russian CBDC legislation expands foreign access" Ledgerinsights.com May 25, 2023.

_____ (2023b) "BIS G20 report explores practical lessons from CBDC projects" Ledgerinsights.com July 11, 2023.

Liu, Z. Z and Papa, M. Can BRICS De-dollarize the Global Financial System? Cambridge University Press (online) Feb. 24, 2022.

Lukonga, I. (2023) "Monetary Policy Implications of Central Bank Digital Currencies: Perspectives on Jurisdictions with Conventional and Islamic Banking Systems" IMF Working Paper WP/23/60. March 2023.

Ma, D. (2021) "Laos central bank to partner with Soramitsu on CBDC study" Centralbanking.com. October 7, 2021.

Ma, J. (2023). "Chinese city of Changshu plans to pay employees using digital yuan" scmp.com. April 23, 2023.

MAS (Monetary Authority of Singapore) (2021). MAS announces 15 finalists for the global CBDC challenge. Media Release. 2021.

Middleton, C. (2023) "BritCoin, ahoy? Digital pound moves into 'design phase', says Bank of England" diginomica.com. May 5, 2023.

MFSM (2016) Manual on Monetary and Financial Statistics and Compilation Guide IMF 2016. Available in multiple languages.

Munster, B. (2019) "EU finance commissioner vows Libra regulation" Decrypt.com. September 13, 2019.

Partington, R. (2021) "Digital currencies pose threat to economy, warns Bank of England" Guardian. June 7, 2021.

PBOC (People's Bank of China) (2021) Progress of Research & Development of E-CNY in China. Report of Working Group on E-CNY Research and Development. July 2021.

Phnompenpost.com. (2022) "Bakong User Numbers Surge" September 29, 2022.

Popper, N. and Li, C. (2021). "China Charges Ahead with a National Digital Currency" New York Times. March 1, 2021.

Prasad, E. (2021) The Future of Money: How the Digital Revolution is Transforming Currencies and Finance (Harvard University Press, September 2021).

Project Aurum (2022) Project Aurum: A prototype for two-tier central bank digital currency (CBDC) Joint project of Hong Kong Monetary Authority, BIS Innovation Hub, and Hong Kong Applied Science and Technology Research Institute. October 2022.

Project Dunbar (2023) "Project Dunbar: International Settlements using multi-CBDCs" BIS.org 2023.

Project Icebreaker (2023) "Breaking new paths in cross-border retail CBDC payments" Joint report by Bank of Israel, Norges Bank, Sveriges Riksbank, and BIS Innovation Hub Nordic Centre. March 2023.

Project Jura (2021) Cross-Border Settlement using Wholesale CBDC Joint project of Banque de France, BIS Innovation Hub, and Swiss National Bank. December 2021.

Project Mariana (2023) "CBDCs in automated market makers" BIS.org 2023.

Project mBridge (2022) Connecting Economies through CBDC Joint Report of Hong Kong Monetary Authority, Bank of Thailand, Central Bank of the U.A.E., Digital Currency Institute of the People's Bank of China, and BIS Innovation Hub Hong Kong. October 2022.

Project Nexus (2023) "Enabling instant cross-border payments" Joint report by the Eurosystem, Malaysia, and Singapore. March 2023.

Pymnts.com. (2021) "El Salvador Pours Bitcoin Profits into Health and Education Amid Ongoing Chivo Wallet Fraud Furor" Pymnts.com. November 5, 2021.

Restofworld.org (2022). "Most Salvadorans have already ditched their national bitcoin wallets" May 4, 2022.

Reuters.com. (2022) "Russia proposes ban on use and mining of cryptocurrencies" Reuters.com. January 21, 2022.

Rösl, G. and F Seitz. (2022) "Central Bank Digital Currency and Cash in the Euro Area: Current Developments and one Specific Proposal" Credit and Capital Markets, Volume 55, Issue 4, April 2022.

Saddam, R.S. (2019) Is the East African Community Ready for a Another Chequered Member? Horninstitute.org December 16, 2019.

SAMA and CBUAE (Saudi Arabia Monetary Authority and Central Bank of the U.A.E.) (2020) Project Aber - Joint Digital Currency and Distributed Ledger Project. 2020.

Schickler, J. (2023) "EU Parliament Passes Bill Requiring Smart Contracts to Include Kill Switch" Coindesk.com March 14, 2023.

Stevens, R. (2020) "Inside the Marshall Islands' New Cryptocurrency: The SOV" Decrypt.com. October 6, 2020.

Strack, B. (2023) "Retail CBDCs Could Pose Risks Not Yet Known, IMF Head Says" Blockworks.co May1, 2023.

Takemiya, M. (2021) "Cambodia's digital currency can show other central banks the way" Paymentsjournal.com. August 30, 2021.

UK Finance (2023) "Unlocking the power of securities tokenization" July 12, 2023.

U.S. President's Working Group on Financial Markets (2021) Report on Stablecoins. November 2021.

World Economic Forum. (2020) Central Bank Digital Currency Policy-Maker Toolkit. January 2020.

Glossary

Algorithmic stablecoins – Stablecoins backed by reserves that use mathematical methods to balance assets to maintain a fixed value.

Altcoins – Alternative coins

AML/CFT (Anti Money Laundering/Countering Financing of Terrorism) – Financial Action Task Force (FATF) rules to detect and report illegal activity.

AMM – Automated Market Maker

API – Application Programming Interface

ASEAN – Association of South East Asian Nations

Bakong – Cambodia CBDC project

BCBS – Basel Committee on Banking Supervision

BIS – Bank for International Settlements

Blockchain – The digital technology that verifies and permanently records transactions in bitcoin and other cryptoassets

BTC - Bitcoin

Byte – Smallest length of computer code needed to represent one character. Code for simple crypto transactions runs several thousand bytes long. Large-scale computer code is measured by Greek prefixes (i.e., gigabyte = 1 billion bytes).

CASP – Crypto Asset Service Provider

CBDC – Central Bank Digital Currency

CD – Capacity Development

Cryptoasset – Any encoded digital financial instrument.

Cryptocurrency – An incorrectly used term for a digital financial instrument intended for use as money. This term is also often loosely used for noncurrency instruments.

CSD – Centralized Securities Database or Depository

DCash – CBDC of Eastern Caribbean Currency Union

DCEP – Digital Currency and Electronic Payment

Defi – Decentralized Finance

Digital asset - Any digital financial instrument.

DLT – Distributed Ledger Technology

DORA – European Union Digital Operational Resilience Act

DTI – Digital Token Identifier

EAC – East African Community

ECB – European Central Bank

ECCU – Eastern Caribbean Currency Union

ECU – European Currency Unit

EMU – European Monetary Union

EU – European Union

FSB – Financial Stability Board

GCC – Gulf Cooperation Council

GSC – Global Stablecoin

EMDE – Emerging Market and Developing Economies

e-cedi – CBDC of Ghana

e-CYN – CBDC of People's Republic of China

e-Money – Any form of electronically recorded value that can be used for transactions by computer, phones, handheld devices, swipe cards, etc.

e-Naira – CBDC of Nigeria

Ethereum – Major altcoin competitor to bitcoin that introduced smart contracts.

FATF – Financial Action Task Force

Fork (and Hard Fork) – A split in a blockchain into two or more chains. A hard fork introduces new blockchain path that does permit return to the old path.

Gwei – A measure of value in the Ethereum system equal to one billionth of an ether.

Halving – Scheduled cuts by half of new bitcoin rewards to miners.

HTLC – Hash Time Locked Contracts

Hub and Spoke – CBDC system shaped like a bicycle tire with central processing hub to which separate national CBDC systems.

ICT – Information and Communication Technology

IMF – International Monetary Fund

IPS – Instant Payment System

ISO – International Organization for Standardization

Irreversibility (of bitcoin etc.) – Transactions cannot be reversed after they are encoded into a DLT block.

JAM-DEX – CBDC of Jamaica

KYC (Know Your Customer) – Supervisory rule that banks must know the true identity of their customers.

m-CBDC Bridge – Project to facilitate international transactions between to different countries' wCBDCs.

MiCA – European Union 'Markets in Crypto-Assets' Regulation

Miners –Global network of independent data processors that create new bitcoins (and other coins) and verify transactions. (Also called 'nodes' or 'validators')

MFSM – IMF Monetary and Financial Statistics Manual

NFT – Nonfungible Token

Nodes – Another term for miner.

130

P2P – Person to Person

Permissioned/Permissionless – Indicates if only authorized validators may operate on a platform, or the platform is open to anyone.

POS – Point of Sale

PQC – Post Quantum Cryptography

Proof-of-stake – System to verify DLT transactions based on consensus of miners based on their financial contribution to system.

Proof-of-work - System to verify DLT transactions based on consensus of miners based on their work involved.

PSP – Payment Service Provider

PvP – Payment-versus-Payment. Under PvP, final payment in a currency is made only if final payment in another currency occurs.

QR code – Quick Response code

rCBDC – retail CBDC

RTGS – Real Time Gross Settlement

Sand dollar – CBDC of Bahamas

Satoshi – One hundred-millionth of a bitcoin = .000,000,01 BTC

Satoshi Nakamoto – Pseudonym of author of 2008 original bitcoin white paper.

Seigniorage – Earnings of the central bank or government from issuing cash and coins,

SEPA – Single European Payments Area

Smart contracts – Instructions built into digital instruments that self activate when specified conditions are met.

Stablecoin – Digital coins designed to have a value equal to a currency or value of other items.

SWIFT – Society for Worldwide Interbank Financial Telecommunications

Throughput – The volume and speed of transactions on a digital platform.

Token (tokenization) – Conversion of financial instruments or assets into digital objects to enable trading via digital channels.

Utility coin – A coin developed for a specific (often proprietary) purpose that often cannot be used outside of its system.

VASP – Virtual Asset Service Provider

Wallet – File for electronic storage of digital assets

WAMZ – West African Monetary Zone

wCBDC – wholesale CBDC.

XC – Exchange and Contracting

XML – eXtensible Markup Language.

Made in the USA
Middletown, DE
30 October 2023

41536066R00076